THE LETTERS OF
Tobias Smollett

TOBIAS SMOLLETT, 1756
By Willem Verelst

THE LETTERS OF

Tobias Smollett

Edited by

LEWIS M. KNAPP

CLARENDON PRESS · OXFORD

1970

Oxford University Press, Ely House, London W.1

GLASGOW NEW YORK TORONTO MELBOURNE WELLINGTON
CAPE TOWN SALISBURY IBADAN NAIROBI DAR ES SALAAM LUSAKA ADDIS ABABA
BOMBAY CALCUTTA MADRAS KARACHI LAHORE DACCA
KUALA LUMPUR SINGAPORE HONG KONG TOKYO

MADE AND PRINTED IN GREAT BRITAIN
BY WILLIAM CLOWES AND SONS, LIMITED
LONDON AND BECCLES

TO
HELEN JUNE KNAPP

PREFACE

S MOLLETT'S letters have been appearing in print gradually for the last two centuries. Many extracts as well as complete letters have been published repeatedly—the usual procedure in the case of eminent authors. In 1769, two years before his death, three of Smollett's letters to John Wilkes were printed in *Letters between the Duke of Grafton . . . &c &c and John Wilkes, Esq. With Explanatory Notes.* In Smollett's *Plays and Poems* (1777), the unknown author of a very brief life of Smollett presented for the first time three of his letters to David Garrick. A few additional letters and extracts were publicized in Dr. John Moore's account of Smollett (vol. i of *The Works of Smollett,* 1797). More appeared in the revised biographies of Smollett in Dr. Robert Anderson's six editions of the *Miscellaneous Works* of Smollett from 1796 to 1820. In his prolonged search for letters, Anderson acquired the manuscripts of eight, six of which he was the first to publish in 1806. In that edition are others printed earlier, as well as sixteen revealing letters addressed to Smollett.

Some half-century later, in 1859, Joseph Irving presented in his *Some Account of the Family of Smollett of Bonhill* extracts from nine letters, then mostly unpublished, sent by Smollett to Dr. John Moore.

In 1926 *The Letters of Tobias Smollett, M.D.,* collected and edited by Edward S. Noyes, Ph.D. were published by the Harvard University Press. This collection contains seventy-four letters, fifteen of which had not been previously printed. It is also an edition with many helpful and scholarly notes.

Dr. L. F. Powell of Oxford discovered seventeen unpublished letters written by Smollett to William Huggins, seven of which appeared in 1936 in *Modern Philology.* The others have become available recently in *Eighteenth Century Studies,* Spiral Press, New York, 1970.

In 1943 Henry W. Meikle, then Librarian of the National Library of Scotland, presented in the *London Times Literary Supplement* 'copies' of seven excellent letters written by Smollett from 1747 to 1754 to his Scottish friend, the Rev. Dr. Alexander Carlyle. In the present edition, however, these letters are based upon the original manuscripts and are for the first time carefully annotated.

In 1950 there appeared the *Letters of Tobias George Smollett, A Supplement to the Noyes Collection,* edited by Francesco Cordasco. In this Supplement are reprints of some twenty-six letters published after Noyes's edition of 1926, as well as five letters which the editor admitted in 1952 to be forgeries. (See *Philological Quarterly*, xxxi (1952), 300, for his statement.)

In the present edition there are one hundred and eight letters. Of course, Smollett must have written scores of notes to his associates who helped him prepare issues of the *Critical Review* and the *British Magazine*, as well as to his publishers. Then there must have been letters to his sister Jane, and to his mother, who lived until 1770. Smollett's available letters are few indeed as contrasted with those of Samuel Richardson, Laurence Sterne, Lady Mary Wortley Montagu, David Garrick, and Dr. Samuel Johnson. They greatly outnumber, however, the amazingly few of Henry Fielding, and amount to about twice as many as those of Oliver Goldsmith.

Despite a very widespread search for hidden and extremely rare letters, there are only three (Letters 19, 99 and 108) now first printed. This edition, however, provides additional and revealing material. There are three postscripts of Smollett's letters to Dr. John Moore which are not included in Noyes's edition. Furthermore, there are in a few letters sentences not found in his edition. There is also an omitted paragraph in Letter 22, one of those sent to the Rev. Dr. Alexander Carlyle, and published from a 'copy' by Henry W. Meikle. Since 1926 when Noyes edited Smollett's letters, much more has been discovered concerning his life, his writings, and his acquaintances, both obscure and prominent. This accumulated information is now carefully utilized in my annotations. It is the hope of all students of Smollett that eventually more of his correspondence will be found.

ACKNOWLEDGEMENTS

As i have been working on the texts and annotations of Smollett's letters for a good many years, it is quite impossible for me to list everyone who has assisted me in preparing this edition. I lack complete records of all the help which I have received from persons in Great Britain, France, Italy, and Jamaica, as well as from my American correspondents. Whether I list them or not I am very grateful to all of them.

I thank the American Philosophical Society for two very helpful grants.

I thank the librarians and their assistants in the following places: The British Museum; The Bodleian Library; The Boston Public Library; The California State Library; The Chelsea Public Library; The Harvard University Library; The Haverford College Library; The Historical Society of Pennsylvania; The Hyde Collection, Somerville, New Jersey; The Henry E. Huntington Library and Art Gallery; The Maine Historical Society; The Massachusetts Historical Society; The National Library of Scotland; The Pierpont Morgan Library; The Mitchell Library, Glasgow; The Norlin Library, University of Colorado; The Princeton University Library; The Public Record Office; The Royal College of Surgeons, London; The Royal Society of Edinburgh; The Tutt Library, Colorado College; The University of Edinburgh Library; The University of Glasgow Library.

I am very grateful also to the following individuals: John Alden, Hugh Amory, Katherine C. Balderston, Roger W. Barrett, Martin C. Battestin, Grace Berger, P. G. Boucé, Col. A. E. Cameron, William C. Coley, James L. Clifford, Lewis P. Curtis, the late Richard A. Ehrlich, Henry L. Fulton, E. A. Hammond, the late R. B. Cunninghame Graham, Robert Halsband, Allen T. Hazen, Frederick H. Hilles, Mrs. Donald F. Hyde, Claude E. Jones, George M. Kahrl, Helen J. Knapp, Hugh H. Knapp, Claire Lamont, Louis A. Landa, Maynard Mack, Louis L. Martz, Lucille Mathias, Alan D. McKillop, the late Henry W. Meikle, Dr. Daniel M. Musher, Winifred A. Myers, Henry J. Pettit, Frederick A. Pottle, L. F. Powell, Reta W. Ridings, James Ritchie, Thomas W. Ross, Hinda Rose, Patrick Telfer Smollett, Marjorie B. Stephenson, Robert W. Taylor, Dorothy Thompson, William B. Todd, Lillian de la Torre, Curt A. Zimanski.

CONTENTS

LIST OF PLATES

Note of Acknowledgement

For permission to publish these portraits I am very grateful to the following owners: Major Patrick Telfer Smollett; owner of the portrait by Willem Verelst. Mr. George Cremer; owner of the portrait by Nathaniel Dance. The National Portrait Gallery; owners of the portrait by an unknown Italian artist.

LEWIS M. KNAPP

ABBREVIATIONS

Anderson	*The Miscellaneous Works of Tobias Smollett, M.D.*, 6 vols. (Edinburgh, 1806), ed. Dr. Robert Anderson, I, 'Life of Tobias Smollett, M.D.'
Anderson (1820)	*The Miscellaneous Works of Tobias Smollett, M.D.*, 6 vols. (Edinburgh, 1820), ed. Dr. Robert Anderson, i, 'Life of Tobias Smollett, M.D.'
BM	British Museum.
BPL	Boston Public Library, Virginia and Richard Ehrlich Autograph Collection.
Carlyle	Dr. Alexander Carlyle, *Autobiography*, ed. John H. Burton (London and Edinburgh, 1910).
Chambers	Robert Chambers, *Smollett* (London and Edinburgh, 1867).
CPL	Chelsea Public Library, London.
DNB	*Dictionary of National Biography.*
HC	Haverford College, Charles Roberts' Autograph Collection.
HCSNJ	The Hyde Collection, Somerville, New Jersey.
HEHL	The Henry E. Huntington Library and Art Gallery.
HSP	Historical Society of Pennsylvania, Du Simitière Papers.
HU	Harvard University, F. Locker-Lampson-Warburg-Grimson album.
Irving	Irving, Joseph, *Some Account of the Family of Smollett of Bonhill; with a Series of Letters Hitherto Unpublished, written by Dr. Tobias Smollett, Author. Arranged by J. Irving* (Dumbarton: Printed For Private Circulation, MDCCCLIX).
Irving (1860)	Irving, Joseph, *The History of Dumbartonshire . . . with Genealogical Notices of the Principal Families in the County.* Second edn. (Dumbarton, MDCCCLX).
JEGP	*Journal of English and Germanic Philology.*
Jones	Claude E. Jones, *Smollett Studies* (University of California Press, 1942).
Kahrl	Kahrl, George M., *Tobias Smollett Traveler-Novelist* (University of Chicago Press, 1945). Reprinted in 1968 by Octagon Books, Inc., New York.
Knapp	Knapp, Lewis M., *Tobias Smollett Doctor of Men and Manners* (Princeton University Press, 1949). Reprinted in 1963 by Russell & Russell, Inc., New York.
Knapp, 'Dissertation'	Knapp, Lewis M., 'A Study of the Final Period of Tobias Smollett: *The Expedition of Humphry Clinker* and Contributions to the Biography of Tobias Smollett and Ann Smollett. A Dissertation presented to . . . Yale University. (1928).

Abbreviations

Martz	Martz, Louis L., *The Later Career of Tobias Smollett* (Yale University Press, 1942). Reprinted in 1967 by The Shoe String Press, Inc., Hamden, Connecticut.
MHS	Maine Historical Society, J. S. H. Fogg Collection.
Mass. HS	Massachusetts Historical Society.
MLN	*Modern Language Notes.*
Moore	Moore, John, M.D., *The Works of Tobias Smollet, M.D.*, 8 vols. (1797), i, 'The Life of T. Smollett, M.D.'
MP	*Modern Philology.*
NLS	The National Library of Scotland.
NQ	*Notes and Queries.*
Noyes	Noyes, Edward S., *The Letters of Tobias Smollett, M.D.* (Harvard University Press, MCMXXVI).
OED	*Oxford English Dictionary.*
PML	Pierpont Morgan Library.
Powell	Powell, L. F., 'William Huggins and Tobias Smollett', *Modern Philology*, xxxiv (1936), 179–92.
PQ	*Philological Quarterly.*
PTS	Manuscripts of Patrick Telfer Smollett.
RCS	Royal College of Surgeons, London, Hunter-Baillie Collection.
RSE	Royal Society of Edinburgh.
TLS	*Times Literary Supplement.*
UEL	University of Edinburgh Library.
UG	University of Glasgow Library.
Whitridge	Whitridge, Arnold, *Tobias Smollett A Study of his Miscellaneous Works* (published by the author, 1925). Reprinted recently by the Folcroft Press, Inc., Folcroft, Pennsylvania.

NOTES ON THE MATERIAL

Letters of Smollett, Unlocated or Destroyed

1740s   Letters to Alexander Leslie, fifth Earl of Leven. (See Letter 7 of this edn.)

1745   A.L.S. 1½ pages, 8vo. to Mr. [William] Hunter, 25 July 1745. 'Smollett is going to Paris and asks for letters of introduction.' Sotheby, 12 Apr. 1875 (John Young Library), item 825. Forster Collection (listed under 'Sotheby') 542, Catalogue 7, in BM.

1749   1 page, 8vo. Sale of F. Naylor's letters by Sotheby, Wilkinson and Hodge, July–Aug. 1885, item 900. Sold to Harvey for £4. 18s. 0d.

c. 1759   Letter to Dr. Alexander Carlyle, alluded to in Dr. William Robertson's letter to Smollett, 15 Mar. 1759. See Anderson, 187–8.

c. 1760   Letter to Admiral Charles Knowles. See Knapp, 232.

c. 1761   Letter to James Boswell. See Frederick A. Pottle, *James Boswell, The Earlier Years 1740–1769* (New York, 1966), 71, 475.

1763   Letter to the Earl of Hertford referred to by Smollett in his letter to Dr. William Hunter, 11 August 1763.

1763   Letter to Mr. Neville referred to by Smollett in his letter to Dr. William Hunter, 11 Aug. 1763.

1769   Letter to W. Kettilby, alluded to by the latter in his letter to Smollett, written at Marseilles, 29 Apr. 1769. MS. of Kettilby's letter at HSP.

1769 (6 Sept.)   Letter to Dr. John Armstrong, alluded to by the latter in his letter to Smollett, written at London, 10 October 1769. MS. of Armstrong's letter at HSP.

c. 1771   Letter to Robert Graham of Gartmore, alluded to by him in his letter to Smollett, written at London, 13 August 1771. See Knapp, 332–3.

Dates unknown   Letters to David Stewart Erskine, eleventh Earl of Buchan. In his letter, 6 June 1806, to Robert Anderson (see MS. 22.4.17, f. 80, in NLS), the Earl of Buchan declared: 'all the letters which passed between the Doctor and myself have been lost or destroyed.'

Dates and Recipients unknown   In Isaac D'Israeli's *The Calamities and Quarrels of Authors* (London, 1859), p. 14, is what appears to be an extract from a lost letter:

Had some of those who were pleased to call themselves my friends been at any pains to deserve the character, and told me

ingenuously what I had to expect in *the capacity of an author, when
I first professed myself of that venerable fraternity*, I should in all
probability have spared myself the *incredible labour and chagrin I
have since undergone.*

In Oliphant Smeaton's *Tobias Smollett* (Edinburgh, 1897), 43,
66, 81, and 95, there are short citations from possibly unpublished letters, one of which (p. 95) is said to have belonged
to one Mr. Goring. All of these may be fabrications. In the
Academy, li (London, 1897), 276, the reviewer of Smeaton's
biography cites from that book (p. 81) the following: 'My life
is sheer slavery; my pen is at work from nine o' the clock the
one morning until one or two the next.'

Forged Letters Attributed to Smollett

See *Letters of Tobias George Smollett A Supplement to the Noyes Collection
with a Bibliography of Editions of the Collected Works*, Collected and
Edited by Francesco Cordasco, Ph.D. . . . (Madrid, 1950):

Letter 19, p. 28
Letter 26, p. 33
Letter 29, p. 35
Letter 30, p. 36
Letter 31, p. 36

Documents Signed by Smollett

Glasgow, 2 May 1738. A bill for clothes. Knapp, 24. MS. at the General
Register House, Edinburgh.

London, 5 May 1753. Smollett's contract to complete for Robert
Dodsley, James Rivington and William Strahan *A New Collection of
Voyages and Travels* before 1 August 1754. Noyes, 23–4. MS. not
located. See *American Book-Prices Current*, 1960–5, Index, p. 2024.

London, 28 Nov. 1753. A receipt of £52. 10s. 0d. to David Wilson and
Thomas Durham for one half of the copyright of Dr. Smellie's second
volume of Midwifery. MS. at HCSNJ.

London, 28 Nov. 1753. A receipt recorded in *The R. B. Adam Library
Relating to Dr. Samuel Johnson and His Era*, 4 vols. (London and New
York, 1929–30), iii, 222. MS. not located.

Chelsea, 12 Nov. 1757. Autograph statement concerning a personal loan,
mentioning Mr. Colquhoun. Knapp, 336.

London, 14 Mar. 1758. A receipt of £20 to James Rivington related to the
copyright of Smollett's *Complete History of England*. This is in addition
to 'upwards of £800' previously received. MS. in the Berg Collection,
New York Public Library.

London, 27 May 1758. Financial statement sent to Alexander Telfer
concerning a payment of £100 to William Strahan. Knapp, 208. MS. in
PML.

Notes on the Material

London, 5 Jan. 1759. Receipt of $7\frac{1}{2}$ guineas for correcting *The Devil on Crutches*. Knapp, 105. MS. at the Bodleian Library.

London, *c*. the end of 1759. Smollett's petition to George II for a royal licence for the sole printing, publishing, and vending of the *British Magazine*. Knapp, 221. MS. in State Papers Domestic, George II, 145, in the Public Record Office, London.

Bath, 14 Mar. 1766. Promissory note of £50 to Robert Smith. MS. in PML.

[London], 1 Apr. 1767. Receipt of £70 to Mr. Hamilton 'for the Copy-Right of the Adventures of Telemachus, translated from the French by me'. Knapp, 'Smollett's Translation of Fénelon's *Telemaque*,' *PQ*, xliv (1965), 405–7. MS. in the Hornby Library, Liverpool.

No place or date. Smollett's signature along with those of Urian Leigh and Richard Ellkin. Knapp, 337, and Lady Charnwood, *An Autograph Collection and the Making of it* (London, 1930), 257.

Editorial Methods

I. *The Printing of the Letters based upon original Manuscripts*

Preceding each letter is the name of the recipient, if known. Otherwise *Anonymous* is printed.

The place where the letter was written and its date, as here printed, are shifted from the end of the epistle to the beginning.

With a few exceptions the manuscript is literally followed. The paragraphs are rarely altered. The spelling and numerals are usually unchanged. However, some abbreviations, including ampersands, are expanded, and elevated letters are lowered except in Smollett's signature, where the T$^{\underline{s}}$ is retained.

The punctuation is, with very few exceptions, modernized: apostrophes are sometimes altered, and periods are substituted for dashes. Capital letters are kept, although it is not always possible to be sure as to whether Smollett penned them. They are added, if necessary, at the beginning of sentences. The square bracket [ ] is used for editorial comment, and the angle bracket, $\langle \ \rangle$, for conjectural reading where a part of the manuscript is missing.

II. *The Printing of Letters, the Manuscripts of which are unavailable*

The texts, published in various places, are reprinted literally with the exception of obvious misprints, and errors in punctuation.

III. *Data immediately following each printed Letter*

The address of the letter, if available.

The present location, if known, of the manuscript.

The location of the first printing of the manuscript. Certainty about this is not always absolute.

The very few postmarks and endorsements on the manuscripts are not included.

INDEX OF CORRESPONDENTS AND LETTERS

Index of Correspondents and Letters

Index of Correspondents and Letters

INTRODUCTION

It is time for a new and complete edition of the letters of the famous Dr. Tobias Smollett.

In these letters, some of them very short and others very long, there is no evidence that he ever thought that they might be published. Some were penned in great haste, but others were carefully written. Their diction is usually quite formal. Many contain colourful and witty details similar to those which enliven his novels and his *Travels through France and Italy*. Notable for lively data are his letters to the Rev. Dr. Alexander Carlyle. No letters to women, except Letter 99, to the Duchess of Hamilton, have been discovered, and in his available correspondence there are no allusions to his courtship, his marriage, his medical practice, his social activities in the London taverns or Chelsea Clubs, or in the Old Chelsea Church.

However, many of his letters contain revealing information. In his correspondence with Dr. George Macaulay, with his brother-in-law, Alexander Telfer, and with Dr. William Hunter, there is much concerning his income from his wife's property in Jamaica, and also several references to uncertain sums coming from the East Indies. Owing to his rather frequent extravagances, such as his travels, dinners for his hack-writers on Sundays, and the cost of his portraits, he often had to borrow money. The paintings included those by Willem Verelst and Nathaniel Dance, both still preserved, and also one by Thomas Gainsborough, and another by Sir Joshua Reynolds, neither of which can be located. It is false, however, to regard him as continually suffering from the hack-writer's poverty.

In the late 1740s he did not allude to financial problems in his long letters to the Rev. Dr. Carlyle, but he expressed his keen interest in current theatrical productions and in his frustrated efforts to stage his own *Regicide*.

Later letters to other friends disclose many details concerning his early novels and his work in *The Critical Review*, as well as the long tasks of his historical writings, and his translations of *Gil Blas* and *Don Quixote*.

Smollett knew some Spanish, although just how much is uncertain. In Letter 43 he cited an unusual Spanish word, and in Letter 89 he referred to his knowledge of that language. In 1764 (Letter 95) he wrote to Dr. William Hunter stating that he hoped to be able to speak Italian 'tolerably in six months' when he planned to visit Italy. He sometimes read Italian with excitement (Letter 66). He must have been able to speak some French, and as a translator of *Gil Blas* he was excellent. In his frequent citations of Latin phrases and sentences he resembled many other writers of his time. It is likely that he sometimes enjoyed reading works in all of these languages as a short respite from his extraordinary amount of varied literary effort.

During his thirteen years in Chelsea he also enjoyed some, albeit brief social activities, for his various attitudes towards the inhabitants of that attractive village on the Thames are expressed in a letter (21) to the Rev. Dr. Carlyle, and also in a very friendly epistle to Dr. Alexander Reid (Letter 93), a prominent English doctor in Chelsea, with whom he probably attended Masonic meetings.

Smollett's closest friends, of course, were Scottish. To Dr. John Moore of Glasgow, his second cousin once removed, he wrote at infrequent intervals fairly intimate letters, all sixteen of which are in this edition. In these he sent his regards and love to his relatives and to his old friends, many of whom were prominent Scottish citizens, and some of whom had been his fellow-students at the University of Glasgow. To several young Scotsmen seeking positions or promotions he was generous in writing notes of recommendation.

Smollett was often too busy or weary to write frequently to his best friends. The hundreds of sheets of handwriting which he sent to his publishers must have exceeded in number those of any other eighteenth-century writer except Defoe. The result of this enormous amount of sedentary toil was prolonged fatigue and illness. In letters to his medical friends and to others, he wrote much about his sickness, remarkable in its fluctuations, and about his many efforts to remedy it by means of travel, sea-bathing, horseback riding, and taking the waters at Bath.

When he wrote one of his letters to Moore in about 1758 (Letter 56), he was so exhausted after correcting his *History of England* that in relation to both the praise and censure he was receiving from his various writings he declared: 'Indeed I am sick of both, and wish to God my circumstances would allow me to consign my Pen to oblivion.' This sentence was quoted by Isaac D'Israeli in his *Calamities of Authors* (the edition printed in New York, 1812, i, 34). In this same volume (p. 32), D'Israeli wrote the following: 'Smollett himself shall be the historian of his own heart . . . and describe that state between life and death, partaking of both, which obscured his faculties and sickened his lofty spirit.' Immediately after this statement is the following sentence in quotation marks, cited apparently from a lost letter of Smollett seen by D'Israeli and written possibly to Dr. John Moore:

'Had some of those who were pleased to call themselves my friends been at any pains to deserve that character, and told me ingenuously what I had to expect in *the capacity of an Author, when I first professed myself of that venerable fraternity*, I should in all probability have spared myself the *incredible labour and chagrin I have since undergone.*'

In Letter 87, sent to Dr. John Moore in the summer of 1762, there is an unusually self-critical confession. Smollett had recently returned from travels in the country and was, he declared, feeling 'perfectly well'. He wrote as follows:

'The Public has always been a liberal Patron to me since I commenced Author. My Difficulties have arisen from my own Indiscretion; from a warm temper easily provoked to Rashness; from a want of Courage to refuse what I could not grant without doing Injustice to my own Family; from Indolence, Bashfullness, and want of Oeconomy. I am sensible of all my Weaknesses. I have suffered by them severely, but I have not Vigour of mind sufficient to reform, and so I must go on at the old rate to the End of the Chapter.'

That he had a 'warm temper' is undeniable, but that he regarded himself to be indolent is amazing! And was he usually bashful? He seems to have been accurate, however, in confessing his lack of 'oeconomy', which in his day meant a frugal use of income.

Other important letters, not usually so autobiographical, are those which Smollett sent to his very hospitable friend, William Huggins, whom he visited several times in Nether Wallop, Hampshire, and to his more prominent correspondents and friends, Samuel Richardson, John Wilkes, David Garrick, John Home, David Hume, William Strahan, Dr. George Macaulay, and Dr. William Hunter.

From the contents of Smollett's letters, as is true even from the hundreds of epistles of other authors, it is difficult to generalize conclusively about his dominant concepts in literary criticism, philosophy, ethics, or religion. The personal convictions of all important writers often evolve with changes throughout their careers. Nevertheless, any careful critic should be familiar with their correspondence in order to secure all possible information about their emotional and intellectual dynamics. Although it is not always done, dealing with these characteristics is as important as the explanations, often expressed in lengthy pedantic terminology, of the author's techniques of characterization and plot-structure.

Smollett's letters ought to be read not only by professional critics but also by the historians of eighteenth-century fiction, who are obliged to allude rather briefly to both a novelist's leading works, and to his personality. It is unfortunate that in recent decades many brief sketches of Smollett's personality are one-sided and erroneous, in view of what his letters reveal. Such portraits are often Victorian, sometimes reflecting what William E. Henley, at the beginning of his Introduction in the first volume of his edition of Smollett's *Works* (1899), declared: 'I purpose . . . to keep as close to the man —the humorous, arrogant, red-headed, stiff-necked, thin-skinned, scurrilous, brilliant Scots hack of genius—as his novels will let me.' Had Henley been able to read more of Smollett's letters, he might not have improvised this prefatory assertion which is itself stiff-necked and not wholly accurate. That Smollett was humorous and brilliant is, of course, true, but that he was red-headed (or that his face was always flushed with rage) is fictional. And he was not a typical eighteenth-century hack writer because in 1760 (Letter 71) he alluded to his amanuensis. Nor was Smollett always violent, arrogant, or scurrilous. Henley included in his edition of Smollett's *Works* an anonymous attack on Fielding in 1752, *A Faithful Narrative of the Base and inhuman Arts That were lately practised upon the Brain of Habbakuk Hilding*. . . . It is possible that Smollett wrote this, but there is no proof that he did so. Such a jocular and incomplete appraisal as Henley's is now quite misleading because in recent decades additional information has been discovered about Smollett's temperament, often choleric and satirical, but often kind and generous.

Such discoveries, now easily available in many of his best letters, elevate his status as a complex but appealing personality, and as a versatile and memorable author.

Letter 1
To James Smollett of Bonhill[1]

Glasgow, April 4th, 1737

Dear Cousin,

I received the enclosed March 25th, in which you will see the motives that induced me to trouble you with this. I would have sent you it ere now, but did not know how to direct for you till Mr. Seton[2] came to this place, and I hope you will be so good as to free my brother[3] from his uncertainty by honouring him with your commands pr. first opportunity, as you will increase the obligations not only of him, but likewise of your most Gratefull

and humble Servt.,
Tobias Smollett

Address: To James Smollett of Bonhill, Esq. to be found at the House of Mrs. M'Gregore,[4] Nidderies Wynd,[5] Edinburghe. *Source:* MS. of PTS. *First Printing:* Noyes, 3.

Letter 2
To ? Mr. Barclay[6] of Glasgow

London, May 22nd, 1744

Dear Sir,

I am this minute happy in yours, which affords me all the satisfaction of hearing from you without the anxiety naturally flowing from its melancholy occasion; for I was informed of the decease of

---

[1] Cousin of Tobias, and head of the family (died 1738).

[2] Possibly William Seton, son of Sir Alexander Seton, first Baronet of Pidmedden. See *Memoirs of the Life of Sir John Clerk of Pennicuik . . .*, ed. John M. Gray (Edinburgh, 1892), 51, n. 2.

[3] James Smollett, who became a Captain in the army and was lost (date unknown) in a naval transport off the coast of America. See Irving, (1860) 343-4.

[4] Unidentified.

[5] A street which extended from High Street to Cowgate.

[6] Robert Barclay matriculated at the University of Glasgow in 1732, became a prominent lawyer in that city, and died at Southampton, 4 Dec. 1783 (Knapp, 19-23).

our late friend by a letter from Mr. Gordon,[1] dated the day after his death.

All those (as well as my dear Barclay) who knew the intimacy betwixt us must imagine that no stroke of fate could make a deeper impression on my soul than that which severs me forever from one I so entirely loved! from one who merited universal esteem; and who, had he not been cut off in the very blossom of his being, would have been an ornament to society, the pride and joy of his parents, and a most inestimable jewel to such as were attached to him, as we were, by the sacred ties of love and friendship. O my dear Ritchie,[2] little did I think at our last parting we should never meet again! How many hours, days—nay, years of enjoyment did I promise myself on the prospect of seeing thee again! How has my heart throbbed at thy imaginary presence! And how oft have I conversed with thee by the indulgence of a dream! Even when I waked to my disappointment, I flew to pleasing hope for refuge, and reflected on the probability of real gratification! But now, alas, even that forsakes me. Hope itself lies buried with its object, and remembrance strives to soothe itself by recalling the delightful scenes of past intercourse! Dear brother, this is a theme I can scarce quit; my imagination broods o'er my melancholy, and teems with endless sentiments of grief and tenderness. My weeping muse would fain pay a tribute to his *Manes*; and, were I vain enough to think my verse would last, I would perpetuate his friendship and his virtue.

As for the particulars you expect from me, you must wait until I shall be better informed myself; for, to tell you an extraordinary truth, I do not know, as yet, whether you had better congratulate or condole with me. I wish I was near you that I might pour forth my heart before you and make you judge of its dictates and the several steps I have lately taken; in which case, I am confident you and all honest men would acquit my principles, howsoever my prudentials might be condemned. However, I have moved into the house where the late John Douglas, surgeon,[3] died, and you may henceforth direct for Mr. Smollett, surgeon, in Downing Street, West.[4] My respects wait on Mr. John Gordon and family; and

---

[1] Dr. John Gordon of Glasgow (?–1772) under whom Smollett served his medical apprenticeship. He received a compliment from Smollett in *Humphry Clinker* (Letter of Bramble from Cameron, 8 Aug.).

[2] John Ritchie (1721–44), son of John Ritchie, merchant of Glasgow. For further data, see Knapp, 23.

[3] John Douglas, a prominent surgeon of Downing Street, died in June 1744. For his obituary and information concerning his distinguished brother, Dr. James Douglas, see Knapp, 47–8.

[4] Westminster.

please let my condolence and best wishes be made acceptable to the parents of my much lamented friend. At the same time, receive yourself the additional portion of affection he possessed in the heart of

Your own,
T.⁵ Smollett

Willy Wood,[1] who is just now drinking a glass with me, offers you his good wishes and desires you to present his compliments to Miss Becky Bogle.[2]

Address: Not available. *Source:* MS. not located. *First Printing:* Robert Chambers, *A Biographical Dictionary of Eminent Scotsmen*, 4 vols. (Glasgow, 1835), iv, 271.

Letter 3

To Alexander Carlyle[3]

[? 1747]

Dr. Carlyle,

Compliments apart, I embrace with Pleasure the Correspondence you proffer and sincerely wish your Expectation may not be disappointed in the Sequel.

I must begin then with a Congratulation on your Change of

[1] Probably William Wood, a factor at the University of Glasgow. See Knapp, 19. This is perhaps the William Wood who entered the University of Glasgow in 1734. See *The Matriculation Albums of the University of Glasgow* (Glasgow, 1913), 13.

[2] Probably a member of the prominent Bogle family of Glasgow, and perhaps related to Robin Bogle of Shettleston, near Glasgow, a friend of Dr. Alexander Carlyle. See Carlyle, *passim.* One George Bogle was Treasurer of Glasgow in 1729; George Bogle of Daldowie was Rector of Glasgow University in 1737–8. See James Cleland, *Annals of Glasgow*, 2 vols. (Glasgow, 1816), i, 191; ii, 116–17.

[3] Dr. Alexander Carlyle (1722–1805) an eminent Scottish minister for over fifty years at Inveresk, a suburb of Musselburgh, near Edinburgh. His autobiography, first published in 1860 and reissued, as edited by John Hill Burton, in 1910, is a fascinating book containing much information about Smollett and his friends. For a short account of Carlyle, see Knapp, 'Early Scottish Attitudes towards Tobias Smollett,' *Philological Quarterly*, xlv (1966), 263–5. Smollett maintained a long friendship with Carlyle, visiting him twice in Inveresk. In Carlyle's papers in the National Library of Scotland is a manuscript catalogue of his library, which contained Smollett's *Roderick Random, Peregrine Pickle, Humphry Clinker,* and the *Continuation of the Complete History of England*.

(3)

To Alexander Carlyle, ? 1747

Character[1] which I pray God, may redound to the Glory of yourself and to the Edification of all about you, although I cannot without Mortification observe a young Fellow of Taste and Spirit, reduced to such a Gothic Dilemma, as will neither permitt Him to improve the One, or indulge the other, but even compell him to Condescensions he can ill digest in espousing Principles he may at bottom disdain; but perhaps my Zeal carries me too far, and there may be Douceurs in the Life of a Scottish Parson which I little dream of. If any thing could Conquer my Antipathy to Sermons (a vulgar prejudice! you will say) it would be the Hope of meeting with something uncommonly Elegant and persuasive in your Compositions; or in those of Dick[2] and some others [of] my Acquaintance, who with a great share of Learning and Taste, have of late undertaken the Ministerial Function. And now we are on this subject, pray let me know if Robt. Paton[3] be settled near you, who was a very honest Fellow when I knew him in London, and of whose Wellfare I am desirous to hear. I am vain of your Approbation with regard to my Tragedy,[4] which, as you imagine, suffered by the much lamented Death of Lord George Graham;[5] tho', after the Assurances I had from many People of much greater Distinction and Influence than he, I little thought my Attempt to bring it on this Season could have been baffled by the Pitifull Intrigues of that little Rascal Garrick, who, at the time he gave me all the Incouragement I could desire, in assuring me he would contribute as much as in him lay, not only to bring it on, but also to act in it with all the ability he was master of, found means to prevail on Rich[6] to reject it. It would much Exceed the Bounds of a Letter, as well as your Patience, to offer a Detail of what passed between him and me on this Score; I shall only inform you that he has served Thomson[7] in the selfsame Manner, which I assure you, has not at all increased the Number of his Friends; and that I account for his Behaviour by the Interest he had in a Comedy which he purchased of one **Dr.**

[1] In the spring of 1747 Carlyle began preaching in several churches, before becoming Minister of Inveresk in 1748.

[2] Probably the Reverend Dr. Robert Dick (1722–82), minister of Grayfriars and later of Trinity College Church, Edinburgh (Harold W. Thompson, *The Anecdotes and Egotisms of Henry Mackenzie* (1927), 258.

[3] In Alexander Carlyle's *Autobiography* there are two references to a Rev. Robert Paton.

[4] *The Regicide.*

[5] The Right Hon. Lord George Graham, son of the first Duke of Montrose, (1715–47). For his obituary see *London Magazine* (Jan. 1747), 53.

[6] John Rich of Covent Garden Theatre. For Smollett's relations with him, see Knapp, *passim.*

[7] James Thomson, the well-known poet and dramatist.

Hoadley,[1] and which has been acted here with great Applause under the Name of the Suspicious Husband, a Piece of Success you will (I believe) wonder at upon reading the Performance.

Meanwhile, I have just finished the Alterations of my Play, as they were agreed upon by the Manager of Drury Lane,[2] who has given his Word and Honour to a Person of Quality that it shall be acted next Winter, at any time before Christmass, that I desire. Bob Smith (a worthy Fellow!)[3] is, as you left him, and John Blair[4] is Tutor to the Children of one Capt. Wilkinson;[5] I cannot say that any Familiarities I entered into with him enabled me to look upon him in a different Light from that in which I considered Him when you was here, and to which you was no stranger. I never heard before, of his Criticism on Othello; and I believe I shall not now importune him much for a sight of it. You raise my Curiosity in mentioning that soliloquy, which I am afraid is not to be had in this Place: and Works of that Kind I am wonderfully fond of. You are as unmercifull in tantalizing me with your own Productions which I insist on perusing. I shall enquire about Home's Essays[6] and doubt not of being entertained by them according to your Progrostic. Mr. Leslie shall be informed of your Misfortune,[7] on which I too condole you. If I had an Opportunity, I would send you the New Play [8] and Farce,[9] Two Satires called Advice and Reproof[10] which made [some Noise here, and a Ballad set to Musick under the name of the Tears of Scotland,[11] a Performance very well received at London, as I hope it will be in your Country which gave Rise to it. The Truth is I have a paternal Concern for that and the Satires

[1] Dr. Benjamin Hoadley (1706–57), physician and dramatist, lived in Chelsea and was author of *The Suspicious Husband*, staged at Covent Garden in Feb. 1747.

[2] James Lacy.

[3] For an account of Robert Smith, see my note, 'Smollett's Friend Smith,' *TLS* (9 Oct. 1943), 492.

[4] Dr. John Blair, LL.D. (?–1782), vicar of Hinckley and prebendary at Westminster. Author of *The Chronology and History of the World* (London, 1754). See *DNB*.

[5] Unidentified.

[6] Probably David Hume's *Philosophical Essays concerning Human Understanding*, first published anonymously, *c.* Apr. 1748. See *The Letters of David Hume*, ed. J. Y. T. Greig, 2 vols. (Oxford, 1932), i, 106, 111.

[7] This may refer to the death of Carlyle's favourite sister in February, 1747. See Carlyle, 209. Mr. Leslie was perhaps John Leslie, son of the tenth Earl of Rothes. See the account of James Graham, first Duke of Montrose in *DNB*.

[8] Probably the revised *Regicide*.

[9] This farce by Smollett has not been located.

[10] Smollett's *Advice* was published in Sept. 1746, and his *Reproof* in Jan. 1747.

[11] See O. E. Deutsch, 'Poetry Preserved in Music,' *MLN*, lxiii (Feb. 1948), 73 ff.

above mentioned, and your Esteem of them is not at all indifferent to

Dr. Sandy,[1]
Yours unaffectedly,
T⁵ Smollett

Address: Not available. *Source:* MS. in NLS. *First Printing: TLS* (24 July 1943), by Henry W. Meikle.

Letter 4
To Alexander Carlyle

[? 1747]

Dr. Carlile,

I own with Shame and Confusion of Face that I have egregiously tresspassed against the Rules of Correspondence in having omitted so long to answer your last. I would have been more punctual had it not been for Oswald the Musician,[2] who promised from time to time to set your Songs to Musick that I might have it in my Power to gratifie the Author in you by sending your Productions so improved. Your gay Catches[3] pleased me much, and the Lamentation of Fanny Gardner[4] has a good deal of Nature in it, tho' in my Opinion it might be bettered. Oswald has set it to an excellent Tune in the Scottish Stile, but as it is not yet published I cannot regale you with it at present. The Satires of which you desired Copies have lain by me these six months, and General Guest[5] being dead, I know not how to Convey them. Since I wrote my last Letter to you, I have finished a Romance in two small Volumes, called the Adventures of Roderick Random, which will be published in a Fortnight.[6] It is intended as a Satire on Mankind, and by the Reception it has met with in private from the best Judges here I

[1] Defined in *OED* as a 'shortened hypocoristic form of Alexander, chiefly used in Scotland'.

[2] See Noyes, 117, and O. E. Deutsch, 'Poetry Preserved in Music. Bibliographical Notes on Smollett and Oswald, Handel and Hayden', *MLN*, lxiii (1948), 73–88.

[3] A musical round in which one singer catches at the words of another, producing ludicrous effects (*OED*).

[4] Not located.

[5] Lieutenant-General Joshua Guest. (*DNB*, and Knapp, 77, n. 27.)

[6] *Roderick Random* was published in Jan. 1748.

(6)

have reason to believe it will succeed very well. As I have long ago disposed of the Copy, I know not what Method the Booksellers will follow in the Sale of it, but I believe some Hundreds will be sent to Scotland. If you shall light on it, read it with Candour, and report me and my Cause aright. I was in hopes of hearing that you were settled in one of the best Livings in Lothian,[1] but I understand the Affair is still undetermined. Remember that (this Letter being only a Confession of my Sins) you are to expect little Entertainment from it. When my Attention shall be less engrossed than it has been for some time past, I will write again; in the mean time if you can spare a few Minutes from Matters of Importance, have Compassion upon me, and oblige with a Letter.

Dr. Sandy,
Your Friend and Servt.,
[T? Smollett]

Address: Not available. *Source:* MS. at NLS. *First Printing:* In *TLS* (24 July 1943), by Henry W. Meikle.

Letter 5

To Alexander Carlyle

London, June 7th, 1748
Dr. Carlyle,

I am so proud of your Panegyrick on Roderick that I can no Longer resist the inclination I feel to signifie how much I am pleased with your Approbation. I have had Occasion to experience that Weakness of Vanity in an Author which exults even in the applause of [a] fool. How much then must I triumph in that Praise which (I flatter myself) is the Result of Veracity and Taste.

In the midst of my Satisfaction (however) at the Success of my Performance, I am not a little mortified to find the Characters strangely misapplied to Particular Men whom I never had the least Intention to ridicule, by which means I have suffered very much in my moral Capacity, some Persons to whom I have been extremely obliged, being weak enough to take Umbrage at many passages of the work, on the Supposition that I myself am the Hero of the Book, and they, of consequence, concerned in the History.

I have heard of Love's[2] Indignation from many hands, and you

---

[1] Lothian, an area including Edinburghshire.
[2] John Love (1695–1750), Smollett's schoolmaster. See *DNB*.

may be sure, treat it with the Contempt it deserves—the more so, as I am informed that he has by way of Revenge propagated many Lies to my Disadvantage.

I shall take this Opportunity therefore of declaring to you, in all the sincerity of the most unreserved Friendship, that no Person living is aimed at in all the first part of the Book; that is, while the scene lies in Scotland and that (the account of the Expedition to Carthagene excepted) the *whole* is not so much a Representation of my Life as of that of many other needy Scotch Surgeons whom I have known either personaly or by Report. The Character of Strap (who I find, is a favourite among the Ladies everywhere) is partly taken from the Life; but the circumstances of his Attachment to Random[1] [are] entirely feigned.

As you have no doubt observed several inaccuracies in the Stile, I must do myself the Justice to assure you that (one or two over-sights excepted) they are all owing to the hurry in which it was printed, and here I am tempted to discover that the whole was begun and finished in the Compass of Eight months, during which time several Intervals happened of one, two, three and four Weeks, wherein I did not set pen to paper, so that a little Incorrectness may be excused.

After having been so tediously impertinent on the subject of Roderick, I will proceed (like a true Author enamoured of the first Person) to inform you that I have contracted with two Booksellers to translate Don Quixote[2] from the Spanish Language, which I have studied some time.[3] This perhaps you will look upon as a very Desperate Undertaking, there being no fewer than four Translations of the same Book already extant, but I am fairly engaged and cannot recede. I will also impart another piece of News which I believe, will surprise you no less, after having perused the Revenge I have taken on the Playhouse Managers in Roderick Random. In short, I have planned a Comedy which will be finished by next winter.[4] Garrick who was inexpressibly galled at the Character of Marmozet,[5] has made some advances towards an Accommodation with me, but hitherto I have avoided a Reconciliation, being deter-

---

[1] Random and Strap are central characters in *The Adventures of Roderick Random*. For persons who may have suggested aspects of the character of Strap, see Knapp, 102.

[2] Smollett's translation, *The History and Adventures of The Renowned Don Quixote*, printed for several booksellers, was first published in Feb. 1755.

[3] How well Smollett knew Spanish is uncertain. See Knapp's review of Carmine Rocco Linsalata's *Smollett's Hoax: Don Quixote in English, JEGP*, lvii (1958), 554–5.

[4] This comedy has never been located.

[5] The character representing Garrick in *Roderick Random*.

mined to turn the Tables upon him, and make him court my good Graces in his turn. You cannot imagine how happy I am made by the account of your Settlement[1] which I hear is one of the best in Scotland. The only Chagrin to which you will be subject must proceed from the Necessity of living under Restraint in the midst of malice and superstition.

I had almost forgot to pique myself upon my Penetration in discovering the Value of Dr. Macghie[2] before you gave me the Hint of his Importance. By what I have observed, he is a man according to my own Heart, and you may be sure I will cultivate his Acquaintance to the uttermost. I shall in a few days have an opportunity of enjoying his Company, in a Partie of Pleasure to Oxford, Blenheim and Stowe; and if I can, will wean him from your old Acquaintance, B—— the wrangler,[3] and others of the same stamp who at present engross him too much. Dr. Carlyle, pardon my Prolixity, and believe me to be in the most genuine Sense,

your Friend, T:ˢ Smollett

Address: Not available.
Source: MS. in NLS. *First Printing:* In *TLS* (24 July 1943), by Henry W. Meikle. Fragments of this letter were published by Henry Grey Graham in his *Scottish Men of Letters in the Eighteenth Century* (London, 1901) 301–2, and by Noyes, 7–8.

Letter 6

To Alexander Carlyle

London, Feby. 14th, 1748/9

Dr. Carlyle,

I am too much perplexed at present to write a Circumstantial Answer to your last, which as usual, gave me abundance of pleasure. A thousand things occur to me, which I would fain communicate; but I must refer them to another Occasion, when you shall receive a Long Letter, the Intention of this being only to assure you that I think of you as often and [as] warmly as ever. I rejoice at your happy Situation [and] at your Complaint as a Lover because [I am] persuaded you will not let yourself sink [upon] any such frivolous Disappointment. I have wrote a sort of Tragedy on the Story of

[1] Carlyle was ordained minister of Inveresk, near Edinburgh, in Aug. 1748, having earlier been assured of this 'settlement' (establishment in a Presbyterian parish).

[2] Dr. William McGhie, Scottish physician and a friend of Carlyle and of Samuel Johnson. For details of his career see Knapp, 80–2.

[3] See Letter 3, n. 4, p. 5, and Carlyle, 353.

To Alexander Carlyle, 14 February 1748/9

Alceste,[1] which will (without fail) be acted at Covent Garden next Season, and appear with such Magnificence of Scenery as was never exhibited in Britain before. Meanwhile, despairing of seeing my old Performance represented, I have at last taken the advice of my Friends, and opened a Subscription for publishing it,[2] which in all appearance will answer my warmest Expectation. Honest Bob Smith[3] is well and pretty comfortably settled within a few miles of London. Gil Blas was actually translated by me,[4] tho' as it was a Bookseller's Job, done in a hurry, I did not choose to put my name to it; however, of three thousand Copies that were printed, scarce 400 remain unsold. Your Advice is extremely judicious, and has all due weight with your Friend, who (notwithstanding) cannot intirely conform to it, for certain Reasons which I will [not] impart at this Juncture. Jack Leslie,[5] without the least provocation, behaved to me one night with such Insolence that had I thought him a proper Object of Resentment, I would have kicked him on the Spot as an unmannerly Jackanapes.

I am with all Sincerit[y] and Esteem,
your Friend and Servt.,
T⁵ Smollett

Who is this Home[6] whom you mention to me as an old Acquaintance? I think I may venture to send my Compliments to him, tho' upon my Soul, I can't recollect any such person. Dr. Macghie[7] is very well—is not this Letter an admirable Composition?

Address: To the Rev^d. Mr. Alexr. Carlyle at Musleburgh near Edinburgh.
Source: MS. in NLS. *First Printing:* in *TLS* (24 July 1943), by Henry W. Meikle.

[1] For his opera, *Alceste*, which was n ever staged, Smollett received on 1 Mar 1749/50 from John Rich £100, a partial payment of the copyright. (British Museum, Egerton MSS. 2269.) John Home stated in an undated letter to Carlyle that Smollett received £300 for *Alceste*. See *The Works of John Home, Esq. . . . to which is prefixed, An Account of his Life and Writings by Henry MacKenzie* . . . 3 vols. (Edinburgh, 1822), i, 137. For the text of the lyrics of Smollett's *Alceste*, see O. E. Deutsch, 'Poetry Preserved in Music', *MLN*, lxiii (1948), 79–85. For other details concerning *Alceste*, see Knapp, 85–91.

[2] No list of subscribers to the edition of *The Regicide* printed for the author in 1749 has been found.

[3] For Robert Smith, see Knapp, 'Smollett's Friend Smith', *TLS* (9 Oct. 1943), 492.

[4] Smollett's translation, *The History and Adventures of Gil Blas of Santillane*, was published in Oct. 1748. For data on its composition and printing, see Knapp, 103–4.

[5] See Letter 3, n. 7, p. 4.

[6] Presumably John Home (1722–1808), a Scottish clergyman, author of *Douglas*, to whom Carlyle gave a letter of introduction to Smollett in 1749. See Letter 7, and Letter 89.

[7] See Letter 5, n. 2, p. 9.

Letter 7
To Alexander Carlyle

London, Octr. 1st, 1749

Dr. Carlyle,

Your Reproach was just; I had absolutely forgot my promise and only remembred that you owed me a Letter, so that you see I have adopted the practice of Life, and can be as Selfish as my Neighbours. If I should pretend to set up in Defence of Tom Jones, in those particulars where he is affected by your Censure, you would easily discover my affectation and be justly offended at my feigned Candour. I will therefore own that the same observations occurred to me which you have communicated, and are indeed obvious to every reader of discernment; even the Author's most sanguine Adherents confess that there is an Evident Difference between that part of his Book which he wrote for the Town, and that which was composed for the Benefit of his Bookseller.[1]

You write so warmly in favour of Mr. Home that I long to be acquainted with him, and hope to be one of the first he shall inquire for on his Arrival at London. I thank you for the Incouragement you shewed to the Regicide which I foresaw would have the Fate you mention, as must be the Case of every Thing of that sort, ushered into the world under the same Circumstances. McGhie[2] (next to Armstrong)[3] is the most reserved Poet I ever met with upon my Soul. I can't reconcile his Shyness in that particular with the Warmth of Friendship he manifests on ever other Occasion. It cannot be Diffidence. I wish it may not be Pride. The Truth is, I am piqued at the Superiority which the Wariness and Wisdom of such Fellows gives them over the weakness and Leakiness of my own Disposition. Yet, notwithstanding, I admire their Conduct, and rejoice at their success. I am told that McGhie is in a very promising way. If I have any opportunity of being acquainted with Lady Lindore[s],[4] you may be sure I shall lay hold on the Occasion and cultivate it accordingly. I was formerly well with My Lord, but our

[1] Lacking Carlyle's criticism of Fielding's *Tom Jones* it is difficult to explain Smollett's statement. By 'Town' he referred perhaps to sophisticated urban readers in contrast to more numerous and less educated readers outside London.

[2] See Letter 5, n. 2, p. 9.

[3] Dr. John Armstrong (1709–79), Scottish physician, poet, essayist, and loyal friend of Smollett. See Knapp, 'Dr. John Armstrong, Littérateur, and Associate of Smollett, Thomson, Wilkes, and other Celebrities', *PMLA* lix (1944), 1019–58. See also Dr. William J. Maloney, *George and John Armstrong of Caselton* (Edinburgh and London, 1954), *passim*.

[4] The wife of Alexander Leslie, fifth Earl of Leven and fourth Earl of Melville.

To Alexander Carlyle, 1 October 1749

Correspondence has been dropt some years. Your Scotch Nobility I have more than once found whimsical and inconstant in their Friendships. Two days Ago, I sent my Masque to Rich,[1] that it may be put into Rehearsal immediately; but he is Such a Compound of Indolence, Worthlessness and Folly, that I cannot depend upon any thing he undertakes. If he acted upon the Maxims of common Sense, tho' he were the greatest Scoundrel under the Sun, I should not have undergone the half of the Trouble I have already suffered; but as his Conceptions are not reducible within any Laws of Reason that I know, his Conduct is altogether unintelligible and his Designs past finding out. Tho' he has no objection to the Piece, which has been again and again approved of by the very Judges he himself appointed; tho' he has no other Prospect of being saved from Destruction than that of exhibiting it immediately; and tho' he is almost certain of uncommon Success on its Appearance, he is such an infatuated Miscreant that he has told some of his friends in Confidence that the Performance was cramm'd down his throat. I may with great Justice say of the Managers, as my Predecessor Michl. Drayton the water poet says of Booksellers—'they are a pack of base Knaves whom I both despise and kick at'.[2]

I have no news wherewith to entertain you, notwithstanding I am but a week returned from having made a Tour thro' part of France, Flanders and Holland,[3] which has only served to Endear my own Country to me the more. Prithee write to me for the future, something oftener than once a twelvemonth and direct for me at the Rainbow Coffeehouse in Lancaster Court by St. Martin's Church.

> I am with great truth and affect[ion]
> Dr. Carlyle, your Friend and Servt.,
> T.[s] Smollett

I have waited 2 posts for a frank[4] because you stand upon such Ceremonies with me, but being disappointed, send it without one.

---

[1] See Letter 3, n. 6, p. 4.

[2] On 14 Apr. 1619, Michael Drayton in a letter to William Drummond of Hawthornden declared: 'the Booksellers and I are in Terms: They are a Company of base Knaves whom I both scorn and kick at.' See the *Works of William Drummond of Hawthornden* (Edinburgh, 1711), folio, p. 153; and Bernard H. Newdigate, *Michael Drayton and his Circle*, (Oxford, Shakespeare Head Press, 1961), 184.

[3] This tour may have included Paris; on 28 Sept. 1749, the Earl of Leven wrote to a friend in Scotland that he had heard that Smollett was then in Paris and that he hoped to meet him. Whether this happened is uncertain (Knapp, 'Early Scottish Attitudes toward Tobias Smollett', *PQ* xlv (1966), 262–3).

[4] See Letter 43, n. 14, p. 61, and postscript.

Address: To the Revd. Mr. Alexander Carlyle Minister of the Gospel at Musselburgh near Edinburgh. *Source:* MS. in NLS. *First Printing:* In *TLS* (24 July 1943), by Henry W. Meikle.

Letter 8

To Francis Hayman[1]

Beaufort Buildings,[2] May 11th, 1750

Dear Sir,

After thanking you heartily for the Trouble you have taken in my Behalf I must beg the additional favour of transmitting my Play[3] to Mr. Garrick, according to his Desire in the Letter which I send you back inclosed, tho' I can forsee that I shall suffer the Mortification of a Second Refusal, which I assure you, I should save myself, but that I am resolved not to be wanting to my own Interest in letting slip any Opportunity (how small soever it may be) of promoting it by just and honourable Means.

In revising and correcting the Performance, I have payed all the Regard to the Patentee's[4] Remarks, which my own Reflection and the Advice of my friends would allow, and made several essential Alterations in the Plan, which he will plainly perceive in perusing it. It cannot be supposed that I would sit down to write a Comedy before I had endeavoured to investigate the nature of the work; or that I am so ignorant of the Stage, so incorrigible, or unqualified as to produce a dramatic piece that should deserve no favour from an audience which never discountenanced any thing that had the least pretension to Encouragement; and yet I have been frustrated in all my attempts to succeed on the Stage, not by the Publick which I have always found favourable and propitious, but by the Power of two or three Persons who (I cannot help saying) have accepted and patronized the works of others, with whom, in point of Merit, I think myself, at least, upon a par. This I speak not from Vanity, but Resentment for the hard usage I have met with. I own

---

[1] Francis Hayman, R. A. (1708–76), a prominent painter, an instructor of Gainsborough, and an important illustrator of books, including Smollett's *Roderick Random*, his translation of *Don Quixote*, and his *Complete History of England*.

[2] Located in Beaufort Street, in the Strand, near the present Savoy Hotel close to the Thames. Smollett lived there from 1748 to 1750.

[3] Probably Smollett's lost comedy, *The Absent Man*, which never appeared on the stage (Knapp, 91–2).

[4] Either James Lacy or Garrick. In 1747 they became co-patentees of Drury Lane Theatre. See *The Letters of David Garrick*, eds. David Little and George M. Kahrl. 3 vols. (Cambridge, Massachusetts, 1963), iii, 1344 ff.

I feel severely when I reflect upon my (I was going to say) unjust Exclusion from the Theatre, but I begin to grow warm, and therefore will conclude with assuring you that I am

Dr. Sir,
    Your obedt. and obliged Servt.,
        T: Smollett

Address: Not available. *Source:* MS. in HU. *First Printing: The Athenaeum*, i (1880), 578.

Letter 9
To John Moore[1]

Chelsea, Septr. 28, 1750

Dr. Sir,

Had it been in my power to serve your Cousin Mr. Fogo,[2] I would have answered your obliging letter immediately upon the receipt of it, but conscious of my Incapacity in that particular, I used the priviledge of my situation and refrained from writing untill I could snatch a vacant hour from the fatigue of my present employment. I thank you for those curious Criticisms on Roderick Random which you have communicated, and congratulate you upon your prospect of enjoying a comfortable settlement among your friends. I have been favoured with two Letters from Mr. Hunter of Burnsyde,[3] the first of which was shewn to the Duke of Dorset[4] by Lady Vane,[5] who spoke of the Author as a Gentleman

---

[1] Dr. John Moore (1729–1802), Scottish physician, novelist, writer of travel literature, and a second cousin once removed of Smollett. He also wrote a biography of Smollett, published in the first volume of his edition of Smollett's *Works*, 8 vols. (London, 1797). See Henry L. Fulton's Dissertation, 'The Making of a Reputation: John Moore, from 1729 to the Publication of Zeluco' (Ann Arbor, Michigan, 1967).

[2] Perhaps William Fogo of Killorn, who married Barbara Anderson; he was imprisoned for debt in the early 1750s.

[3] David Hunter of Burnside, a Jacobite. For references to him see David, Lord Elcho, *A Short Account of the Affairs of Scotland in the Years 1744, 1745, 1746* (Edinburgh, 1907), *passim*.

[4] Lionel Cranfield Sackville, first Duke of Dorset (1693–1768), was Lord President of the Privy Council in 1750.

[5] The Viscountess Vane, *née* Frances Anne Hawes (1713–88), wife of William Holles, Viscount Vane. Her memoirs, published in *Peregrine Pickle*, were perhaps revised by Smollett. See Rufus D. S. Putney, 'Smollett and Lady Vane's Memoirs', *PQ* xxv (1946), 120–6. For information about Lady Vane, see Knapp, *passim*, and James L. Clifford's notes in his edition of *Peregrine Pickle* (Oxford University Press, 1964).

worthy of the Government's Clemency and Protection, and represented his Case and Character in such an advantageous Light that
the Duke expressed an Inclination to befriend him, and advised
Lord Vane to speak to his Cousin the Duke of Newcastle[1]
in his behalf. This Task his Lordship has undertaken, and there
the affair must rest 'till the King's Return. Make my Compliments acceptable to your Mother, and take it for granted that
I am

your sincere friend and humble servt.,

T͜S Smollett

Address: To Mr. John Moore Surgeon at Glasgow pr. Edinburgh. *Source:*
MS. of PTS. *First Printing:* Partly printed by Irving, 18; Noyes,
10–11.

Letter 10

To William Hunter[2]

Rainbow Coffeehouse, Monday, Octr. 15, 1750

Dr. Prof,

I called at your house in hopes of getting a dinner, bu[t] my
principal Design was to desire you will appoint a meeting with Drs.
Smellie[3] and Pitcairn,[4] and I shall take care to attend you. Peter

---

[1] Thomas Pelham-Holles, first Duke of Newcastle (1693–1768), was Lord
Vane's cousin. In 1750 he was Secretary of State for the Northern Department,
and was later Prime Minister. For many years he controlled ecclesiastical
patronage. He was conspicuously eccentric and the constant butt of satires,
such as *The History of Tom Dunderhead* (London, 1750), and Smollett's
laughable portraits of him in *Humphry Clinker* (Letters of Jery, 2 June and
5 June).

[2] Dr. William Hunter (1718–1783), brother of John Hunter, the surgeon, and
a celebrated Scottish physician and lecturer on anatomy. He collected material
now in the Hunterian Museum at the University of Glasgow. He was one of
Smollett's loyal friends in London for some twenty-five years.

[3] Dr. William Smellie (1697–1763), the very prominent obstetrician and
close friend of Smollett. By 1750 Smollett was preparing for the press Smellie's
first publication, *A Treatise on the Theory and Practice of Midwifery* (1751). For
further details concerning their friendship, see Knapp, 139–40.

[4] Dr. William Pitcairn (1711–91), physician at St. Bartholomew's Hospital,
1750–85, and President of the College of Physicians, 1775–85. For a revealing
account of his activities and personality see Carlyle, 349 ff. For his portrait and
further details, see Dr. William Macmichael's *The Gold-Headed Cane* (New York,
1932), Ch. IV.

(15)

Gordon[1] shall wait on you tomorrow to receive your directions on that subject, and I am

Yrs etc.,

T˰ Smollett

Address: To Mr. Wm. Hunter Surgeon in Covent Garden. *Source:* MS. at UG. *First Printing:* Most of it appeared in Thomas H. Bryce's pamphlet, 'William Hunter and His Museum' (Glasgow, 1922), 13. The complete text was published in Knapp, 137.

Letter 11

To [William] Hunter

[*c.* 1750]

Mr. Professor,

Louttit[2] was with me on Saturday last, earnestly solliciting my Interest with Dr. Pitcairn in behalf of his Boy, who is (it seems) a miserable object, afflicted with scorbutic, lep'rous, or scrophulous ulcers, for which he desires the child should be admitted in Bartholomew's Hospital. Such Admission would be an act of charity (I'm afraid) on more accounts than one; and I doubt not but the Doctor, out of his own humanity, will be ready to befriend him, especially when recommended by you.

Louttit has been advised to have Recourse to the Doctor by a Gentleman belonging to the Hospital, who assures him that the Boy will be admitted, should our Friend make a Point of it, tho' otherwise, objections might be made to his Reception on account of the Circumstances of the Disease. In the name of God, use your Influence with the Doctor; for Louttit is very clamorous and importunate, and will consider the favour as an indelible obligation. As you will probably see him soon, take some method of letting me know whether or not the Boy can be

---

[1] An obscure hack writer and possibly a schoolmaster. In 1752 Gordon, having refused to repay money lent him by Smollett, was attacked by him. This resulted in a court trial (H. P. Vincent, 'Tobias Smollett's Assault on Gordon and Groom' *RES* xvi (1940), 183–8). See Letter 15, n. 4, p. 51.

[2] Probably the apothecary referred to in 'A Letter from Andrew Reid, Esq. to Dr. Wilmot, concerning the Effects of Tonquinese Medicine', London, 1745, and printed in *The Philosophical Transactions of the Royal Society of London . . . Abridged,* vol ix (London, 1809), 89–93. See *The Matriculation Albums of the University of Glasgow* (Glasgow, 1913), for two students named Louttit. One was 'Gulielmus Louttit', who enrolled in 1733; the other was 'Jacobus Louttit' of Glasgow, who enrolled in 1737. Smollett probably knew one or both of these as a fellow-student.

admitted on Wednesday, which I hear is the Doctor's taking-in Day.

Yours,

T.⁵ Smollett

Whence all those petulant queries upon the Margins of Smellies Manuscript?[1] have we not Hiren here?[2]

Address: To Mr. Hunter Surgeon at his House in Covent Garden. *Source:* MS. at HEHL. *First Printing:* By Knapp in *MLN*, xlviii (1933), 246–7.

Letter 12

To [William] Hunter[3]

[*c.* 1751–2]

Dear Hunter,

I have been hedging and lurching[4] these Six weeks in expectation of that cursed ship from Jamaica, which is at last arrived without Letter or Remittance.[5] I do not know whether God will have it that you should endure the Persecution of my wants without flinching, or that I should at length tire you out, and be shaken off at once, but, certain it is, I am at present, in consequence of little Demands which I have put off to the last day of Procrastination, in absolute necessity of eight or ten pieces,[6] without which I can no longer answer the Occasions[7] of my Family. This Declaration is by God himself! like wormwood and Brimstone to me, and were myself alone concerned, I would rather perish than have Recourse to such beggarly Sollicitation. For heaven's sake, do not look upon me as one of those Sneaking Rascals who can stoop to subsist upon what

---

[1] While preparing Smellie's manuscript for the press, Smollett had apparently shown it to Dr. William Hunter.

[2] This alliterative query is a line spoken by Pistol in Shakespeare's *Henry IV Part II* (II, 4, 172 and 189). The line is thought to have been in a lost play by George Peele, *Turkish Mahomet and Hyrin the fair Greek.* See *Hiren* in *OED.* The word *Hiren* [or *Irene*] came to mean a strumpet or harlot (E. Cobham Brewer's *The Reader's Handbook of Allusions, References, Plots and Stories,* Philadelphia, 1880). As spoken by Pistol, the word *Hiren* seems to have been a pun, meaning an iron sword or Peele's Hyrin. Prompted by Hunter's petulant queries, Smollett's comic question has similar connotations.

[3] See Letter 10, n. 2, p. 15.

[4] Dodging and remaining secretly in some places like a bankrupt trying to escape being arrested. A humorous statement in this context.

[5] Income from Mrs. Smollett's property in Jamaica (Knapp, 326–8).

[6] Guineas, or gold coins worth twenty-one shillings in the eighteenth century.

[7] Needs.

(17)

they can borrow without shame, Remorse, or purpose of Repayment. I am an unfortunate Dog whose Pride Providence thinks proper to punish with the Tortures of incessant Mortification; and I resent my Lot accordingly. But in the midst of those miserable Littlenesses to which my Destiny drives me, I am still with a due Sense of the Predicament in which I stand.

Yours etc.,
T^s Smollett

I yesterday sent Gordon[1] to David Wilson[2] for a small supply, and find the Creature has been in Holland these ten days, so that I am compelled in this manner to add a Load to your Difficulties; for, if you was a man of Fortune, I could apply to you without Reluctance or Apprehension.

Address: Not available. *Source:* MS. at RCS. *First Printing:* In article by Victor G. Plarr in the *British Medical Journal* (22 Oct. 1904). Plarr omitted the postscript.

Letter 13
To Mr. Richard Oswald[3]

Chelsea, Feby. 11th, 1752

Sir,

Upon the Supposition that you wish me well, I take the Liberty to explain my present Situation, and make a proposal which I hope you will see no Cause to reject. You will easily believe that the Expense of housekeeping,[4] added to my former occasions[5] and incumbrances, must have thrown me considerably back in a course of

---

[1] Probably Peter Gordon. See Letter 10, n. 1, p. 11.

[2] The bookseller, D. Wilson, who sold the copies of the first edition of *Peregrine Pickle* (1751). See *A Dictionary of the Printers and Booksellers . . . in England . . . from 1726 to 1775*, eds. Plomer, Bushnell, and Dix (Oxford University Press, 1932) 266, where it is stated that he was located at Plato's Head near Round-Court in the Strand. On the title-pages of the first edition of *Peregrine Pickle*, his name appears: 'Printed for the Author: And sold by D. Wilson, at Plato's Head, near Round-Court, in the Strand.'

[3] Presumably Richard Oswald (1705–84), see *DNB*. Oswald was an important Scottish merchant in London who had also lived in America and in Jamaica. He and David Maccollo (see n. 1, p. 19) were in charge of Mrs. Leaver's property in Jamaica. Oswald was a friend of Benjamin Franklin and chief commissioner for peace negotiations at Versailles in 1782.

[4] Samuel Johnson limited his definition of *housekeeping* to 'hospitality; liberal and plentiful table'.

[5] Needs.

four or five years during which I touched not one farthing from Mrs. Leaver.[1] Accordingly my Debts in London amounted to about £300, when her last Remittance arrived. Out of the money she drew from your hands, she, without being asked, presented me with two hundred pounds, a sum which was barely sufficient to quiet the most clamorous of my Creditors; and the Rest I put off untill she should recieve [sic] the next Remittance of £200, which you know Mr. Bontein[2] promised to send in six weeks from the Date of his last letters. We have waited for this Supply several months beyond the time he fixed; and now that my necessities recur, I am deterred from applying to Mrs. Leaver for these Reasons. She is naturally obstinate, narrow minded, and totally ignorant of Life, and after having so lately given me two hundred pounds which she looks upon as an infinite Sum, she would be alarmed and frightened almost out of her Senses at a fresh Demand, and conclude that I am either a Spendthrift or in Debt, for which Reason, she might, in the Disposal of her Effects, take measures to cut off all my Expectations; her fears and Suspicions would be communicated to her Daughter; a Breach between the mother and me would probably ensue, and the Peace of my family be utterly destroyed; whereas, by leaving everything to her own generosity, I may be enabled gradually to extricate myself from my Difficulties, provided her Agent shall discharge his Trust like a man of Honour; for, by his own Reckoning, he ought by this time to have a thousand pounds of her money in his hands. What I therefore propose, and would recieve as an indelible obligation is that you would oblige me with one hundred pounds of her money which is in your hands in order to satisfy Demands which are at present extremely pressing, and take my note payable upon Demand for that Sum, or if you desire it, Mr.

[1] Mrs. Elizabeth Leaver, Smollett's mother-in-law, died in 1762 and was buried in Chelsea Old Church.

[2] Thomas Bontein, second son of Mr. Bontein of Boglass in Stirlingshire, and cousin of the father of Robert Graham of Gartmore, who, upon inheriting Bontine of Ardock's estate assumed for a time the name of Bontine, a surname not to be confused with Bontein (see a manuscript letter from Professor William Richardson to Smollett's biographer, Robert Anderson, M.D., in the National Library of Scotland, MS. 22.4.13, ff. 134–134ᵛ). Thomas Bontein held public offices in Jamaica, including that of the Clerk of the Court in Kingston (R. B. Cunninghame Graham's *Doughty Deeds* (London, 1925), 19, 38, and 86). Smollett, in his will, dated 24 Aug. 1769, named Thomas Bontein, along with Robert Graham and others, as one of his executors, not knowing that Bontein had died. In the *London Chronicle* (17–19 Oct. 1769), 382, is the following: 'Kingston, July 22. A few days ago died at his penn [*penn* is a word used in the West Indies and meaning *plantation*, or *country house*] near Salt Ponds, Thomas Bontein, Esq; a Gentleman who had filled several public offices in this island.'

Maccullo[1] will join in the Security. Upon my honour! I should never dream of asking this Favour were I not certain of your being indemnified at all events. In all Likelihood, you will never be without some of Mrs. Leaver's Cash in your hands, as she has no earthly occasion for money except to defray the Expence of boarding her Grandchild,[2] which does not amount to Thirty pounds a year; and she told me that as her money was much safer in your hands than at home, she had no thoughts of removing it. But should she ever be disposed to draw for the whole, if I cannot easily refund it on Such an Occasion, I will, at least, take the whole of it upon myself, and plead Necessity in my own Excuse. If I were connected with a Sensible woman, who would cordially interest herself in my affairs and behave with that openness and Candour which I deserve at her hands, I should not be driven to the necessity of these dissagreable Expedients, but I have too much Reason to say she is reserved, distrustfull, and as timorously cautious, as if she believed herself environed with Thieves and Ruffians. Whatever Reasons you may have to decline my Request, I beg you will not expose to any unconcerned Person the nakedness of my Situation as I have here displayed it because what I have said is in full Confidence of your honour and Discretion.

I am, Sir,
your very humble Servt.,
T: Smollett

Address: To Mr. Richd. Oswald Mercht. in London. *Source:* MS. at HC. *First Printing:* Noyes, 11–13. The contents were summarized in a catalogue by Willis and Sotheran (1856), and reprinted by Chambers, 87n.

Letter 14
[To Daniel MacKercher][3]

Chelsea, Friday Feb. 23d, 1753

Dear Sir,

I shall take it as a particular favour if you will peruse the inclosed

---

[1] David Maccullo (or Macculloch) referred to as both an apothecary and a surgeon in St. Martin-in-the-Fields, London. See Letter 31, and Knapp, 286, 328. According to John Gray in his letter to Smollett, written in London, 8 July 1771, 'Dr. Macculloch' returned to Ayr after visiting London that summer, and after enquiring about Smollett.

[2] Frances Lascelles, granddaughter of Elizabeth Leaver, who bequeathed her 'one hundred pounds Jamaica currency'.

[3] Daniel MacKercher (*c.* 1702–72), a lawyer. See Knapp, 121, n. 72 for a summary of his interesting associations and activities.

rough draft of a letter which I intend to send to Mr. Hume Campbell,[1] provided you think it contains nothing actionable.[2] I hope you will excuse this trouble, and believe me to be with equal sincerity and attachment,

Dear Sir,

Your very humble Servant,

T. Smollett

Address: Not available. *Source:* MS. not located. *First Printing: European Magazine,* v (1784), 169. It was sent to the *European Magazine* by G. H., who in a preliminary note asserted it was written to Daniel MacKercher.

Letter 15

[To Alexander Hume Campbell][3]

[Chelsea, Friday, Feb. 23d, 1753]

Sir,

I have waited several days in hope of receiving from you an acknowledgement touching those harsh, unjustifiable (and let me add) unmannerly expressions which you annexed to my name in the Court of King's Bench, when you opened the cause depending between me and Peter Gordon ;[4] and as I do not find that you have discovered the least inclination to retract what you said to my prejudice, I have taken this method to refresh your memory, and to demand such satisfaction as a gentleman injured as I am has a right to claim.

The business of a Counsellor is, I apprehend, to investigate the truth in behalf of his Client; but surely he has no privilege to blacken and asperse the character of the other party without any

[1] Alexander Hume Campbell (1708–60), twin-brother of Hugh Campbell, third Earl of Marchmont. (*Marchmont and the Humes of Polworth,* (Edinburgh, 1894), 107–8.) Alexander Hume Campbell was M.P. for Berwickshire and was appointed Lord Clerk Register in 1756. In Hogarth's print, 'Paul before Felix', published in May 1751, Tertellus is said to be a satirical portrait of Hume Campbell, notorious for his coarse language as a lawyer (*Hogarth's Graphic Works,* compiled by Ronald Paulson, 2 vols. (Yale University Press, 1965), i, 215–16).

[2] Containing grounds for legal action.

[3] See n. 1, above.

[4] For Peter Gordon, see Letter 10, n. 1, p. 16. See also H. P. Vincent, 'Tobias Smollett's Assault on Gordon and Groom', *RES,* xvi (1940), 183–8. Exactly when the case between Smollett and Gordon here referred to was opened is not clear, and how Gordon could have afforded to have Hume Campbell for his lawyer is very strange.

(21)

regard to veracity or decorum. That you assumed this unwarrantable privilege in commenting upon your brief I believe you will not pretend to deny when I remind you of those peculiar flowers of elocution which you poured forth on that notable occasion. First of all, in order to inspire the Court with horror and contempt for the Defendant, you gave the Jury to understand that you did not know this Dr. Smollett; and, indeed, his character appeared in such a light, from the facts contained in your brief, that you never should desire to know him. I should be glad to learn of what consequence it could be to the cause whether you did or did not know the Defendant, or whether you had or had not an inclination to be acquainted with him? Sir, this was a pitiful personality, calculated to depreciate the character of a gentleman to whom you was a stranger, merely to gratify the rancour and malice of an abandoned fellow who had feed you to speak in his cause. Did I ever seek your acquaintance, or court your protection? I had been informed, indeed, that you was a Lawyer of some reputation, and, when the suit commenced, would have retained you for that reason had not I been anticipated by the Plaintiff; but, far from coveting your acquaintance, I never dreamed of changing a word with you on that or any other subject. You might therefore have spared your invidious declaration until I had put it in your power to mortify me with a repulse, which, upon my honour, would never have been the case, were you a much greater man than you really are.— Yet this was not the only expedient you used to prepossess the Jury against me. You was hardy enough to represent me as a person devoid of all humanity and remorse, as a barbarous ruffian, who, in a cowardly manner, had with two associates as barbarous as myself called a peaceable gentleman out of his lodgings, and assaulted him in the dark, with intent to murder. Such an horrid imputation publickly fixed upon a person whose innocence you could hardly miss to know is an outrage, for which, I believe, I might find reparation from the law itself, notwithstanding your artful manner of qualifying the expression by saying *provided the facts can be proved.* This low subterfuge may, for aught I know, screen you from a prosecution at law, but can never acquit you in that Court which every man of honour holds in his own breast. I say you must have known my innocence from the weakness of the evidence which you produced, and with which you either was or ought to have been previously acquainted, as well as from my general character and that of my antagonist, which it was your duty to have learned. I will venture to say you did know my character, and in your heart believed me incapable of such brutality as you laid to my charge. Surely, I do not over-rate my own importance in affirming that I am not so obscure in life as to have escaped the notice of Mr. Hume Campbell; and I will be bold enough to challenge him and the whole world to prove one instance in which my integrity was called, or at least left, in question. Have not I, therefore, reason to suppose that in spite of your own internal conviction, you undertook the cause of a wretch, whose ingratitude, villany, and rancour are, I firmly believe, without example in this kingdom; that you magnified a slight correction bestowed by his benefactor, in consequence of the most insolent provocation, into a deliberate and malicious scheme of assassination; and endeavoured, with all the virulence of defamation, to destroy the character, and even the life, of an injured person, who, as well as yourself, is a gentleman by birth, education, and profession? In favour of whom, and in consequence of what,was all this zeal manifested, all this slander exhausted, and all this scurrility discharged? Your Client, whom you dignified with the title of Esquire, and endeavoured to raise to the same footing with me in point of station and character, you knew to be an abject miscreant whom my compassion and humanity had lifted from the most deplorable scenes of distress; whom I had saved from imprisonment and ruin; whom I had cloathed and fed for a series of years; whom I had occasionally assisted with my purse, credit, and influence. You knew, or ought to have known, that, after having received a thousand marks of my benevolence, and prevailed upon me to indorse notes for the support of his credit, he withdrew himself into the verge of the Court, and took up his habitation in a paltry alehouse, where he not only set me and the rest of his creditors at defiance, but provoked me by scurrilous and indecent letters and messages to chastise him in such a manner as gave him an handle for this prosecution, in which you signalized yourself as his champion for a very honourable consideration. There is something so palpably ungrateful, perfidious, and indeed diabolical, in the conduct of the Prosecutor, that, even in these degenerate days, I wonder how he could find an Attorney to appear in his behalf. O Tempora! O Mores! After having thus sounded the trumpet of obloquy in your preamble, and tortured every circumstance of the Plaintiff's evidence to my detriment and dishonour, you attempted to subject me to the ridicule of the Court by asking a question of my first witness, which had no more relation to the cause than if you had desired to know the name of his grandmother. What title had you to ask of a tradesman, if he knew me to be an Author? What affinity had this question with the circumstances of the assault? Was not this foreign to the purpose? Was it not impertinent, and proposed with a view to put me out of countenance, and to raise the laugh of the spectators at my expence? There, indeed, you was disappointed, as you frequently are in those little digressive efforts by which you make yourself remarkable. Tho' I do not pretend to possess that superlative degree of effrontery by which some people make a figure at the bar, I have assurance enough to stand the mention of my works without blushing, especially when I despise the taste, and scorn the principles of him who would turn them to my disgrace. You succeeded, however, in one particular; I mean, in raising the indignation of my Witness, of which you took all imaginable advantage, puzzling, perplexing, and brow-beating him with such artifice, eagerness, and insult, as overwhelmed him with confusion, and had well nigh deprived me of the benefit of his evidence. Luckily for me, the next gentleman who was called confirmed what the other had swore, and proved to the satisfaction of the Judge and Jury, and even to your own conviction, that this terrible deliberate assassination was no more than a simple blow given to a rascal after repeated provocation, and that of the most flagrant kind; that no advantage was taken in point of weapons; and that two drabs, whom they had picked up for the purpose, had affirmed upon oath a downright falsehood with a view to blast my reputation. You yourself was so conscious of this palpable detection that you endeavoured to excuse them by a forced explanation, which, you may depend upon it, shall not screen them from a prosecution for perjury. I will not say that this was like patronizing a couple of Gypsies who had forsworn themselves, consequently forfeited all title to the countenance, or indeed forbearance of the Court; but this I will say, that your tenderness for them was of a piece with your behaviour to me, which I think was equally insolent and unjust; for, granting that you had really supposed me guilty of an intended assassination before the trial began, you saw me in the course of evidence acquitted of that suspicion, and heard the Judge insist upon my innocence in his charge to the Jury, who brought in their verdict accordingly.[1] Then, Sir, you ought in common justice to have owned yourself mistaken, or to have taken some other opportunity of expressing your concern for what you had said to my disadvantage, tho' even such an acknowledgement would not have been a sufficient reparation because, before my witnesses were called, many persons left the Court with impressions to my prejudice, conceived from the calumnies which they heard you espouse and encourage. On the whole, you opened the trial with such hyperbolical impetuosity, and conducted it with such particular bitterness and rancour that everybody perceived you was more than ordinarily interested; and I could not divine the

[1] Though found innocent of 'intended assassination', Smollett was not acquitted of assault (Vincent's article, Letter 15, n. 4, p. 21).

mysterious bond of union that attached you to Peter Gordon, Esq. until you furnished me with the key to the whole secret by that strong emphasis with which you pronounced the words, Ferdinand Count Fathom. Then I discovered the source of your goodwill towards me, which is no other than the history of a law-suit inserted in that performance, where the author takes occasion to observe that the Counsel behaved like men of consummate abilities in their profession, exerting themselves with equal industry, eloquence, and erudition, in their endeavours to perplex the truth, brow-beat the evidence, puzzle the Judge, and mislead the Jury.[1] Did any part of this character come home to your own conscience? or did you resent it as a sarcasm levelled at the whole Bench without distinction? I take it for granted this must have been the origin of your enmity to me because I can recollect no other circumstance in my conduct, by which I could incur the displeasure of a man whom I scarce knew by sight, and with whom I never had the least dispute, or indeed concern. If this was the case, you pay a very scurvy compliment to your own integrity by fathering a character which is not applicable to any honest man, and give the world a handle to believe that our Courts of Justice stand greatly in need of reformation. Indeed, the petulance, licence and buffoonery of some Lawyers in the exercise of their function is a reproach upon decency, and a scandal to the nation; and it is surprising that the Judge, who represents his Majesty's person, should suffer such insults upon the dignity of the place. But whatever liberties of this kind are granted to the Counsel, no sort of freedom, it seems, must be allowed to the Evidence, who, by the bye, are of much more consequence to the cause. You will take upon you to divert the audience at the expense of a witness by impertinent allusions to some parts of his private character and affairs; but if he pretends to retort the joke, you insult, abuse, and bellow against him as an impudent fellow who fails in his respect to the Court. It was in this manner you behaved to my first witness, whom you first provoked into a passion by your injurious insinuations; then you took an advantage of the confusion which you had intailed upon him; and lastly, you insulted him as a person who had shuffled in his evidence. This might have been an irreparable injury to the character of a tradesman, had not he been luckily known to the whole Jury, and many other persons in Court, as a man of unquestioned probity and credit. Sir, a witness has as good a title as you have to the protection of the Court, and ought to have more because evidence is absolutely necessary for the

---

[1] The last part of this sentence is quoted *verbatim* from Smollett's *Ferdinand Count Fathom*, Ch. XXXVII. There is further satire on law and lawyers in Chs. XXII and XXXVI.

investigation of truth; whereas, the aim of a Lawyer is often to involve it in doubt and obscurity. Is it for this purpose you so frequently deviate from the point, and endeavour to raise the mirth of the audience with flat jokes and insipid similes? or, have you really so mistaken your own talents as to set up for the character of a man of humour? For my own part, were I disposed to be merry, I should never desire a more pregnant subject of ridicule than your appearance and behaviour; but, as I am at present in a very serious mood, I shall content myself with demanding adequate reparation for the injurious treatment I have received at your hands; otherwise I will in four days put this Letter in the press,[1] and you shall hear in another manner—not from a ruffian and an assassin—but from an injured gentleman, who is not ashamed of subscribing himself,

[T.̇ Smollett]

Address: Not available. *Source:* MS. not located. *First Printing:European Magazine,* v (1784), 169–71.

Letter 16
[To Daniel MacKercher]

Monday Morning
[*c.* Feb. 1753]

Dear Sir,

I am much mortified that my rascally situation will not at present permit me to send more than the trifle inclosed,[2] as nothing could give me more pleasure than an opportunity of shewing with how much friendship and esteem

I am, dear Sir,
Yours most faithfully,
T. Smollett

Address: Not available. *Source:* MS. not located. *First Printing:European Magazine,* v (1784), 171.

[1] This letter has not been found in the newspapers of 1753, and it is likely that, following MacKercher's advice, Smollett did not send it to Alexander Hume Campbell.

[2] Perhaps a small sum of money sent to MacKercher in gratitude for his advice, which was, very likely, not to send Letter 15 to Alexander Hume Campbell.

Letter 17
To Dr. George Macaulay[1]

Chelsea, May 27, 1753

Dear Sir,

I yesterday met with Provost Drummond[2] and took my leave of him after we had settled the manner of executing his brother's work.[3] At parting, he told me that he left the whole to my management, and that he would entirely acquiesce in whatever I should claim by way of acknowledgement for my trouble. About a fortnight ago he gave me leave to draw upon him for fifty guineas at one month after date, and as I had occasion for the money, I gave a discount for the note at the rate of 60 per cent. Such an unconscionable premium, you may be assured, I should not have given unless upon an emergency, which would admit of no delay: the term was begun, and I was obliged to pay the costs and damages of that scoundrel Groom,[4] according to the compromise made in court. The other fifty guineas, I expect, will be earned in less than a month, and though Mr. Drummond desired me to write to him from time to time, I would not appear so meanly impatient as to demand this second moiety until he himself shall think proper to mention it. Nevertheless, I am so straitened in consequence of that bankruptcy, by which I lost 180 l., the lawsuit with Gordon and his

---

[1] Dr. George Macaulay (*c.* 1716–66), husband of the celebrated historian, Catharine Macaulay, was a successful Scottish obstetrician and Treasurer of the Brownlow Lying-In Hospital in Brownlow Street, Long Acre, near Drury Lane, London. He was repeatedly generous in helping Smollett cope with financial difficulties, as is shown in Smollett's letters to him down to 1759. Macaulay must have had a comfortable income as he lived in Jermyn Street, and in 1766 in St. James's Place (*London Chronicle* (16–18 Sept. 1766), 274). In Oct. 1765, he and his wife arrived in Bath along with Smollett and Mrs. Smollett (*Pope's Bath Chronicle*, 17 Oct. 1765). Among Macaulay's other friends were Drs. John and William Hunter, and Dr. William Smellie.

[2] George Drummond (1687–1766), Lord Provost of Edinburgh six times from 1725 to 1763. See William Baird's account of him in *The Book of the Old Edinburgh Club* (Edinburgh, 1911), IV, 1–54. He was Grand Master of the Free Masons of Scotland and a prominent and very influential citizen, who contributed much to the improvement of Edinburgh. For an engraving of George Drummond, see *Scots Magazine*, lxiv (1802), opposite p. [357].

[3] *Travels through different Cities of Germany, Italy, Greece, and Several Parts of Asia, as far as the Banks of the Euphrates: in a Series of Letters* . . . By Alexander Drummond, Esq; His Majesty's Consul at Aleppo. London, Printed by W. Strahan for the Author, 1754. Alexander Drummond was the British Consul at Aleppo from 1754 to 1756. For a very favourable review of his book (much revised in view of the fact that Smollett received 100 guineas for his ghostwriting) see the *Monthly Review*, xi (1754), 198–211.

[4] For Groom, see Letter 10, n. 1, p. 16.

accomplices, the want of punctuality in our Jamaica agent, and the time I have lost during these six months past, that I must be fain to raise this second payment per advance if I can find any friend who will do me the favour. To you I should have applied myself, without scruple or remorse, had it not been for that 15 l. which has lain over so long; though my delay in that particular was as much owing to my confidence in your friendship, as to the disappointments I have sustained; and I must still beg your patience, until the arrival of the Kingston ship, which is daily expected, and in which Mr. Bontein[1] has solemnly promised to remit what is due us from Jamaica; he is now accountable for above 1000 l. With regard to the 50 guineas, which I very much want, I would much rather owe the favour to you than to any other person; and I would take it upon that footing, which would, in some measure, alleviate the mortification I have in putting you to such trouble; that is, I should be glad, and indeed insist upon paying interest for the money, as well as for that which I already owe. Yet I am afraid it may not suit your convenience to comply with my request, as I know you have already launched out considerable sums of ready money for the relief of your neighbours in distress.

Dear Doctor, this sort of communication is a troublesome tax, imposed upon those who maintain connexions with the needy; and, by Heaven! I despise myself for being obliged to run such risques of cooling that friendship which hath already so warmly interested itself in behalf of, dear Sir, your much obliged and affectionate humble servant,

T? Smollett

Address: Not available. *Source:* MS. not located. *First Printing: Scots Magazine* (May 1804). This text follows that of Anderson, 175–6.

Letter 18

To Alexr. Telfer of Symington, Esqr.[2]

Chelsea, Decr. 13th, 1753

Dear Sir,

I have felt incredible Vexation and Disturbance of Mind about that last money I drew for, because the Sum arising from the Sale of Lands in the Merse[3] upon which I had the security is still de-

[1] See Letter 13, n. 2, p. 19.

[2] Smollett's brother-in-law.

[3] The Merse (or Marsh) is a section in the southern part of Berwickshire (*Blue Guide to Scotland*, ed. L. Russell Muirhead, fourth ed. (London, 1959), 2).

tained by some formality of the Law; however, as I have been very importunate with the Person in whose favour I drew he has yesterday given me as a collateral Security, a Draught upon a Banker in London, from a Gentleman of Sussex, for £130. of the money, which draught will be payed from the first of the Sale of certain Lands which the Chancellor has permitted him to alienate for his sister's Portions, so that it is impossible that I should be a Loser in the End, tho' the Payment has been so long delayed. For this Reason I have enabled myself to take up your Draught upon me by drawing again at two months; and when you shall redraw upon me at the same date, your Bill shall be punctually honoured. By these means I gain four months more, and the Person whose Security I have defrays the Expence of Exchange.

I expect every day to hear from France in answer to the Letters which were written concerning the Lead,[1] and I shall immediately intimate to you the Accounts I receive. Be so good as tell my aunt, Mrs. Bethune,[2] that Jamie[3] is come to London, and I shall take care of him, and let Mr. Moffat[4] know that I have received his Letter by Mr. Ainzlie[5] whom I will introduce to Mr. Miln,[6] the merchant, on Sunday Evening. By the bye, Mr. Miln has in partnership with another friend of mine got five thousand pounds in the Lottery.[7] John Sutherland's Sister[8] has thrown him wholly upon my hands, on pretense of her being incapable of serving him, and this I will say for him, that in five or six days after he set out for Kent, he returned to my House with as much indifference as if it had been his own Home. I have introduced him to the Secretary of the African Company, who has promised to use his influence in his behalf, and I hope he will soon be provided for. I ought to make a thousand apologies for the repeated Freedoms I have taken with your good nature and Friendship, but upon my Soul! I want words to express

[1] In 1753, Alexander Telfer was leasing with great profit lead mines at Wanlockhead, Dumfriesshire, although his financial connection with France is obscure. See Donald MacLeod, *Ancient Records of Dumbarton* (Dumbarton and Glasgow, n.d.), 121–2. See also Rev. J. Moir Porteous, '*God's Treasure-House in Scotland,*' *A History of the Times, Mines, and Lands in the Southern Highlands* (1876), 79.

[2] Jean, daughter of Sir James Smollett, married John Bethune, collector of customs in Kirkcaldy.

[3] Probably one of Smollett's cousins.

[4] Unidentified.

[5] Perhaps John Ainslie, tutor in 1766 of Richard Oswald, Jr., son of Smollett's merchant-friend Richard Oswald.

[6] Probably the Mr. Milne of Letter 34.

[7] For the national lottery of 1753 drawn 26 Nov. 1753, see John Ashton, *A History of English Lotteries* (1893), 69.

[8] Unidentified.

my Sense of Gratitude and Shame so that you must put the most favourable Interpretation on my silence, and allow me to be with unutterable affection and Esteem,

Dear Sir,

your most obliged Brother and Servt.

T.^s Smollett

Present my Love and best Respects to my Mother, Sister, Aunt Nelly,[1] Mrs. Bethune, Miss Jeany and Miss Mary Telfers,[2] Mr. and Mrs. Moffat, Bob Muschet[3] and the two Miss Campbells,[4] and let me not be forgot by Sandy and Jamie[5] when you see them.

Address: Alexr. Telfer of Symington Esqr. To the Care of Mr. Edward Lothian, Goldsmith in the Parliament Close, Edinburgh. *Source:* MS. of PTS. *First Printing:* Noyes, 27–8, incomplete.

Letter 19
To John Moore[6]

Chelsea, Jany. 21, 1754.

Dear John,

Perhaps I should not yet have answered your Letter by Mr. Fogo[7] unless this opportunity had occurred of writing by Mr. Straton,[8] whom I must recommend to your Acquaintance and Friendship, not only as a young Gentleman of Probity and Good Sense, but as the Partner of our friend and Townsman Tom Harvie,[9] with whom he has engaged in Business as a Chymist and Druggist. You may remember I bespoke your Custom for these Gentlemen when I saw you at Glasgow, but your Imagination was at that time so much engrossed by other Ideas that in all probability you have forgot my

[1] Probably Mrs. Dugald Campbell (*née* Elinor Smollett), aunt of Tobias Smollett. She married Dugald Campbell of Craignish in 1718. See Irving (1860), 342.

[2] Probably Smollett's nieces.

[3] Possibly related to Dr. William Muschet, a member of the Royal College of Physicians, 1767.

[4] Perhaps the daughters of Mrs. Dugald Campbell, Smollett's cousins.

[5] For Jamie, see n. 3, p. 29.

[6] See Letter 9, n. 1, p. 14.

[7] See Letter 9, n. 2, p. 14.

[8] Unidentified.

[9] Probably Dr. Thomas Harvie, who obtained his M.D. from the University of Glasgow in 1755 (W. I. Addison's *Roll of the Graduates of the University of Glasgow*).

Recommendation which I must now beg leave to repeat in the strongest terms because I am sure you will find your account in complying with it; for, you may depend upon being served with great care and fidelity at a very moderate Expence. You may likewise influence your friends of the Profession to deal with them.

Your cousin Fogo, who is a very pretty young fellow, has sailed, I believe, by this time, and, I dare say, will (if he lives) be a Credit to his family. I wish it had been as much in my power as it was in my Inclination to befriend him. I am pleased to find you have dissengaged yourself from a Connexion which might have been productive of dissagreable Consequences, and hope you will be more inquisitively cautious for the future. Indeed, I wish you uninterrupted Prosperity in all your undertakings, and am with my best Respects to your Mother, Sister and all friends,

Dear John,
Yours Sincerely,
T. Smollett

I lately saw a Letter from St. Christophers[1] to John Lewis, Bookbinder of Chelsea,[2] written by one of the Executors of Tom Lewis,[3] who says that the said Tom had left his whole Fortune to James Tennant,[4] except a Legacy to Dr. John Muir of Glasgow[5] tho' I believe Jas. Muir[6] is the person meant. You may inquire about the affair. My Compts. to your Partner,[7] Dr. Dick,[8] Bob Barclay,[9] Will Wood,[10] and all friends at Glasgow.

[1] Saint Christopher (or Saint Kitt's), a small island in the British West Indies.

[2] Smollett's neighbour and friend, whom he referred to as 'alias Strap' in Letter 39. It is strange that Thomas Faulkner and later historians of Chelsea have furnished considerable information about this person, apparently under the name of William Lewis. (Thomas Faulkner, *An Historical and Topographical Description of Chelsea and its Environs*, 2 vols. (Chelsea, 1829), i, 170–1). It is possible that this bookbinder was named John William Lewis. Faulkner lived for seven years with Lewis's widow. In her obituary in the *Gentleman's Magazine*, lxvii (Mar. 1797), 252, it is stated that her husband died in 1783, that he was the original of Strap in *Roderick Random*, and that he dined every Sunday with Smollett.

[3] A bookbinder listed in Ellic Howe, *A List of London Bookbinders 1648–1815* (London, 1950), 59.

[4] Unidentified.

[5] Unidentified.

[6] Possibly the surgeon, James Muir of Glasgow (John Glaister's *Dr. William Smellie and his Contemporaries* (Glasgow, 1894), 283).

[7] Thomas Hamilton, Professor of Anatomy and Botany in the University of Glasgow.

[8] Dr. Robert Dick, M.D., Glasgow, 1751, son of Mr. Robert Dick, Professor of Natural Philosophy at the University of Glasgow.

[9] Robert Barclay (Letter 2, n. 6, p. 1).

[10] William Wood (Letter 2, n. 1, p. 3).

Address: Not available. *Source:* MS. of PTS. *First Printing:* In this edition.

Letter 20

To John Moore

Chelsea, March 1, 1754

Dear John,

By this time I suppose you have received a Letter from me, by Mr. Straton,[1] which will give you all the Information ~~which~~ [*sic*] I can impart with regard to Tom Lewis's Legacy,[2] tho' I am afraid it was designed for Mr. Jas. Muir,[3] with whom I understand he had some Connexion.

Mr. Urie[4] is misinformed about my Intention to publish any thing upon Commerce, which is a Subject quite foreign to my Taste and Understanding. I suppose the Mistake arose from my having translated a Collection of Essays[5] from a periodical work published in French under the Title of *Journal Oeconomique* in which there are some papers upon Trade, but this is no other than a paultry Bookseller's Jobb, in which my name ought not to be mentioned.

I have nothing ready for the Press but Doctor Smellie's second volume containing Cases in Midwifery,[6] and my Translation of Don Quixote which will be published next year.[7] I have likewise made some Progress in the History of the German Empire,[8] which I believe will be printed this ensuing summer; and Drummond's Letters[9] are now ready to appear.

In short, dear John, I am so jaded that I now write with infinite Reluctance, so that you must excuse my inaccuracy to all other defects in

Your affectionate humble servt.,
Ts Smollett

[1] Unidentified.

[2] Not located. See Letter 19, n. 3, p. 31.

[3] Letter 19, n. 6, p. 31.

[4] Robert Urie (*c.* 1711–71), an excellent printer in Glasgow before the days of the Foulis brothers. See Hugh A. McLean's 'Robert Urie, Printer in Glasgow', *Records of the Glasgow Bibliographical Society*, iii, session 1913–14 (Glasgow, 1915), 89 ff.

[5] *Select Essays on Commerce, Agriculture, Mines, Fisheries and other Useful Subjects* (London, 1754). This volume contains 39 essays on a variety of subjects, comprising 516 pages. This translation must have kept Smollett very busy for many hours.

[6] *Collection of Cases and Observations in Midwifery* (London, 1754).

[7] Smollett's translation was published in Feb. 1755.

[8] A section of the modern part of the *Universal History*.

[9] See Letter 17, n. 3, p. 27.

Present my best Wishes to your mother and sisters, and let me be kindly remembered by Doctors Dick, and Hamilton,[1] your Partner, Urie, Barclay,[2] Blackburn,[3] and all friends at Glasgow.

Address: Mr. John Moor, Surgeon in Glasgow, North Britain. *Source:* MS. in BPL. *First Printing:* Irving, 18, incomplete; Noyes, 28–9.

Letter 21

To Alexander Carlyle

Chelsea, March 1, 1754

Dear Carlyle,

I do not think I could enjoy Life with greater Relish in any part of the world than in Scotland among you and your Friends, and I often amuse my Imagination with schemes for attaining that Degree of Happiness, which, however, is altogether out of my Reach. I am heartily tired of this Land of Indifference and Phlegm where the finer Sensations of the Soul are not felt, and Felicity is held to consist in stupifying Port and overgrown Buttocks of Beef, where Genius is lost, Learning undervalued, and Taste altogether extinguished, and Ignorance prevails to such a degree that one of our Chelsea Club asked me if the weather was good when I crossed the Sea from Scotland, and another desired to know if there were not more Popes than one, in as much as he had heard people mention the Pope of Rome, an Expression which seemed to imply that there was a Pope of some other Place. I answered that there was a Pope of Troy, and another of Tartary, and he seemed perfectly well satisfied with the Information, which no Person present pretended to contradict.

The same Stolidity prevails among the audience of our Theatres so that I am not very sorry for the Dissapointment of Hume,[4] whom I love exceedingly. Goody Criticism has been delirious a long time, but now she is quite lethargic, so that an Author who formerly went to hell in the thunder and whirlwind of a Riot is now negatively damned, and silently sinks into oblivion. The third night of Constantine[5] did not pay the Expence of the House; think on that,

---

[1] See Letter 19, n. 7, p. 31. [2] See Letter 2, n. 6, p. 1.

[3] Hugh Blackburn, merchant (Noyes, 138–9).

[4] John Home (1722–1808), the dramatist, was repeatedly disappointed by his failure to have his plays staged in London in the 1750s, before his successful *Douglas* was produced there in 1757.

[5] A play by the Rev. Philip Francis. Smollett is accurate in his report on its third performance (*London Stage*, Part IV, ed. G. W. Stone, Jr., (Carbondale, Illinois, 1962), p. 411).

To Alexander Carlyle, 1 March 1754

Master Brooke![1] think on that and tremble. The holy Cross could not save him. It was no longer *hoc signo vinces*, but *hoc signo moriturus es*.[2] The Town puts me in mind of a huge Serpent of Ceylon[3] that gorged itself with a Tyger untill it became quite stupid and insensible. The English Audience hath been crammed with new Tragedies untill it spues again; hence proceeds a Loathing which would reject the most delicate Entertainment of that species. Indeed they have not Sense enough left to distinguish between Draff[4] and Dainties. This, then, must be an unlucky period for Authors of Genius. You exclaim O Boadicia![5] have you read Philoclêa?[6] ola![7] You will by and by see Virginia,[8] ah! ah! but there is another Virgin of the same name,[9] tho' indeed by this time she is an old maid, reserved in Petto[10] by a very curious fellow, one John Moncreif formerly Purser of a Man of War.[11] God grant that she may not be once more murthered by her own father. He is a

---

[1] Probably Henry Brooke (?1703–83), a minor dramatist, author of *Gustavus Vasa*, and of novels, including the *Fool of Quality*. See Oliver Elton, *A Survey of English Literature 1730–1780*, 2 vols. (London, 1928), i, 238–41.

[2] Translated, the Latin means: by this sign thou shalt conquer . . . by this sign thou art about to die.

[3] Smollett is apparently referring to some account or print of a Serpent of Ceylon, which I have not located.

[4] Dregs.

[5] Richard Glover's tragedy, *Boadicea*, 1753. A second edition of this play was published in Dec. 1753, by Robert Dodsley.

[6] McNamara Morgan's tragedy, *Philoclea*. Extracts from this play were published in the *Universal Magazine*, xiv (Feb. 1754), 70–81.

[7] An Anglicized spelling of the Spanish exclamation, *olé*, meaning *bravo*!

[8] Samuel Crisp's *Virginia*, 1754. See Letter 22. This tragedy, staged at Drury Lane on 25 Feb. 1754, had a very short run. For Garrick's prologue and epilogue to it, see Mary E. Knapp, *A Checklist of Verse by David Garrick* (University of Virginia Press, 1955), p. 52.

[9] About 1754 there were three tragedies written, all containing heroines named Virginia: Samuel Crisp's *Virginia*; John Moncreiff's *Appius*; and Mrs Frances Brooke's *Virginia*, not staged, but published in Dublin in 1754, and in London in 1756, and favourably reviewed in the *Critical Review* (Apr. 1756), i, 276–9. For a detailed account of these three plays, see *The Early Diary of Frances Burney, 1768–1778*, ed. Annie Raine Ellis, 2 vols. (London, 1913), ii, 325–32. For Crisp's *Virginia*, see *The Letters of David Garrick*, eds. Little and Kahrl, 3 vols. (Harvard University Press, 1963), Letter 844.

[10] This phrase means undisclosed.

[11] John Moncreiff (?–1761), author of *Appius*, and, among other publications, a few essays on the navy. In a copy of his *Camillus A Dialogue on the Navy* in the British Museum, there is a short anonymous manuscript account of his life. According to this, he was a Scottish tutor (at sea) of a 'son of Mr. Cockburn, Lord of the Admiralty' and later the tutor of one Mr. Ryder at Eton, who upon the death of his father, Sir Dudley Ryder, made a settlement of £100 a year on Moncrieff, for life. This anonymous account concludes by stating that Moncreiff died in 1761 at York on his way to Scotland.

most turbulent Patriot and swears he will make a Turnpike Road to the stage. Methinks I see him with a Collar of Tickets collecting Toll for the support of this *Via Asinorum*. I hope he will settle it at a small rate, or else take orders on the third night. I lately insulted Andrew Millar[1] with the enterprizing Spirit of our friend Gavin Hamilton,[2] and he had nothing to say but that he knew the Bargain before I spoke. His manner of answering from the Purpose is a Figure in Dialogue[3] which I have often known used with great Success. I think it was Melvil[4] who one Evening asked of Ebenezer Young[5] if ever he had known an honester fellow than Bob Elliott,[6] to which Interrogation the said Ebenezer replied with some precipitation, 'by God I was at his Mother's Burial'.

The Proposals for my Translation of Don Quixote are now printed,[7] and what with the new Cutts and the Paper, it will make a very grand Appearance. I have likewise prepared Smellie's Second Volume of Midwifery for the Press,[8] and believe my History of the German Empire[9] will be printed sometime in Summer, so that you see I am not idle. By this time, doubtless you have heard that all our Endeavours in behalf of Smith[10] miscarried through young Shaw-field's[11] aversion to a Tutor. He must be a youth of promising parts who knew Bob personally and rejected him as a Companion. I am glad of our Friend's Disappointment in that quarter because in all probability he will be settled here to his Satisfaction in another family. Every thing is in an excellent Train so that he can scarce fail of Success, and I believe you will have the pleasure of seeing him in a very little time. You will be joyous and happy, and my Spirit will be among you. Tell Jack Hume[12] I think he might find Leisure to visit me in a Letter. Make my Compts. to Mr. Cardonnel,[13]

[1] Andrew Millar (1706–68) was a Scotsman, and one of the leading London booksellers and publishers for some forty years. Though he did not publish Smollett's novels he received a compliment from Smollett in his *Continuation of the Complete History of England*, iv, 129 n. For Millar's career, see *A Dictionary of the Printers and Booksellers*, eds. Plomer, Bushnell and Dix (Oxford University Press, 1932), 171–3.

[2] Gavin Hamilton, prominent bookseller and printer in Edinburgh, *c.* 1733–66. In 1754, his business enterprise was rewarded by the fact that his firm was appointed printers to the University of Edinburgh.

[3] An unusual rhetorical expression.

[4] Unidentified.   [5] Unidentified.

[6] Possibly a relative of Sir Gilbert Elliot.

[7] Copies of these Proposals have disappeared.

[8] See Letter 20, n. 6, p. 36.   [9] See Letter 20, n. 8, p. 32.

[10] Robert Smith (Letter 3, n. 3, p. 5).

[11] Unidentified.   [12] John Home, author of *Douglas*.

[13] Mansfeldt Cardonnell, a Commissioner of the Customs in Scotland. In Smollett's *Humphry Clinker*, Bramble was pleased to drink tea with him (Letter of Bramble, Edinburgh, July 18).

and the honest Parsons to whom you introduced me—I mean Jardan,[1] Logan,[2] Blair[3] and Hepburn,[4] and when you are not better employed, send another long Letter for the Amusement of

Dear Carlyle,

yours ever,

T. Smollett

I have seen Doctor Dixon,[5] who seems to be an honest fellow, and I will cultivate his acquaintance accordingly. Maghie[6] like Truth has prevailed at last. Have you seen a Poem called Taste?[7] I think there is stuff[8] in it, and suspect that Armstrong has stole it upon the Public by which it is neglected.

Address: Not available. *Source:* MS. at NLS. *First Printing: TLS* (31 July 1943), by Henry W. Meikle.

Letter 22
To Alexander Carlyle

Chelsea, April 15th, 1754

Dr. Carlyle,

I snatch the first Opportunity I can find to answer your Letter because Time is precious to your friend in whose behalf you ask my advice. His disorder is certainly no other than a weakness or relaxation of the seminal parts occasioned perhaps by a superpurgation[9] or an excessive discharge from the Glands of the Urethra after a

[1] Probably the Rev. John Jardine, a minister at Edinburgh, whom in 1763 Boswell described as 'a hard-headed, jolly dog'. See *Boswell's London Journal*, ed. Frederick A. Pottle (1950), p. 282.

[2] The Rev. George Logan, minister at Ormiston, near Edinburgh.

[3] Probably Hugh Blair, D.D. (1718–1800) (Robert Morell Schmitz, *Hugh Blair* (King's Crown Press, New York, 1948)).

[4] The Rev. Thomas Hepburn (?–1777). (Carlyle, 279.)

[5] Probably Thomas Dickson, later Alexander Carlyle's brother-in-law (Carlyle, *passim*). Dickson became physician at London Hospital in 1759 and was called by Smollett to attend his daughter Elizabeth in her final illness in 1763.

[6] Dr. William McGhie (Letter 5, n. 2, p. 9).

[7] Dr. John Armstrong's *Taste: An Epistle to a Young Critic* was published in London in 1753.

[8] *Stuff*, as used here, may mean good material, but in Johnson's *Dictionary* fourth ed. (1773), it is stated that stuff 'is now seldom used in any sense but in contempt or dislike'.

[9] The bad effects of excessive purges were stressed by Dr. William Fordyce. See his *A Review of the Venereal Disease and Its Remedies* (London, 1772), 35–6.

venereal Complaint in a Scorbutic habit.[1] The only Indication of Care,[2] therefore, is to strengthen the parts, correct the Acrimony of the Juices, and prevent the patient from committing any excess either of repletion or evacuation, which might strain the Vessels or disorder the Circulation. Let him first be blooded in the Arm and ⟨every⟩ day take a dose of Manna[3] with Cremor Tartan.[4] Then he may begin to take every morning for a fortnight or three weeks about a Gill of the expressed Juice of [MS. torn] oreum and Becabunga[5] mixed with a small wine Glass full of white wine. After this Course it will be proper to take for Breakfast a quarter of an ounce of Isinglass[6] dissolved in a pint of milk and sweetened with sugar; and this ought to be continued for several weeks. In the meantime, let his Loins be covered with a defensative Plaister spread upon Leather and supported by a Bandage; let his Diet be nourishing, comprehending Sago[7] and strengthening Jellies. Let his Exercise be moderate, and he must wholly abstain from venery and hard drinking. His Blood being corrected and inspissated[8] by the Juices and milk, he may have Recourse to the Bark[9] and the cold Bath provided his Lungs be perfectly free from all Complaints; he may drink moderately of Claret, and three or four times a day use an injection of it, mixed with an equal Quantity of a strong decoction of oak Bark. The best way ⟨of taking⟩ the Cold Bath is to plunge Headlong every morning into a Tub full of water, and [MS. missing] mediately, but, if he cannot find a wooden Bath for the purpose, he may [take] himself to the Sea. The Plaister must not be neglected, and if Acids are ⟨not disag⟩reable I would advise

[1] Scorbutic constitutions, i.e. physical constitutions susceptible to scorbutic diseases.

[2] It is possible to indicate a brief appraisal of Smollett's list of prescriptions. Dr. Daniel M. Musher of the New England Medical Center Hospitals in Boston, Massachusetts, has examined the following books: W. Cockburn's *The Symptoms, Nature, Cause and Cure of Gonorrhoea* (London, 1718); William Fordyce's *A Review of the Venereal Disease, and Its Remedies* (London, 1772); and John Hunter's *A Treatise on the Venereal Diseases*, second ed. (London, 1788). On the basis of statements in these books, Dr. Musher believes that, with a few exceptions, Smollett's 'Concept of the pathophysiology of gonorrhea as suggested by the few lines we have is extraordinarily primitive'. Furthermore, Smollett does not mention, as do Fordyce and Hunter, the use of mercury as a primary method of therapy.

[3] Vegetable sugar.

[4] Cream of Tartar.

[5] An herb of the genus Veronica (Veronica Beccabunga).

[6] A semi-transparent form of gelatin.

[7] Sago, or Sagu, a kind of jelly obtained from palm-trees, and apparently related to the modern pudding, sago.

[8] Thickened.

[9] Probably Peruvian bark.

him to swallow half a Gill of distilled Vinegar every day an hour or more before Dinner.

I condole with you upon the Death of poor Logan,[1] who seemed to be an amiable young fellow; and sincerely sympathize with Home in the Loss of his Brother,[2] whom I had the pleasure of knowing. I know what a man of Jack's sensibility must feel upon such an occasion; for I once sustained the same Calamity, in the Death of a Brother whom I loved and honoured.[3]

Bob Smith[4] sets out this very day for Galloway[5] to take upon him the Charge of superintending the Education of Lord Gairlies,[6] in which I hope God will prosper his Endeavours. From Galloway he will repair to Glasgow, so that I believe you will not see him in his Passage, whatever desire he may have to be among you. Perhaps he may contrive a Meeting, and, at any rate, he will write you an account of his Situation. I am glad to hear the Bleacher[7] has come off the field so clean, and long to see his production. Crisp's Virginia[8] was acted with Applause, tho' John Moncreif[9] says the Author has left the subject untouched; indeed these two Gentlemen treat one another with great Contempt. Crispe, being one Evening at Strahan's[10] said he had seen a Gentleman at Lord Coventry's house,[11] who in giving an Account of Moncreif's performance, observed that Appius, the Decemvir,[12] says very deliberately upon seeing the deplorable fate of Virginia, 'the man has killed his Daughter',[13] upon which his Lordship suggested that the Expression would have been raised, had he added, 'God damn my Blood if he has not!' Crispe, who repeated this Remark with great pleasantry, seems to have taken the Hint, for he has made his

[1] For details concerning the death of the Rev. George Logan in Feb. 1754, see Carlyle, 314–15.

[2] David Home, brother of John Home, died in Feb. 1754. See the reference in n. 1.

[3] James Smollett. See Letter 1.

[4] Smollett's friend, Robert Smith (Letter 3, n. 3, p. 5).

[5] Located in Southern Scotland in Kirkudbrightshire.

[6] Probably John Stewart, Lord Garlies, seventh Earl of Galloway, born in 1736. Boswell dined with him and his wife in London at a large social breakfast and concert in 1762 (*Boswell's London Journal*, ed. Frederick A. Pottle (New York, n.d.), p. 70).

[7] Dr. Francis Home, author of *Experiments on Bleaching* (Edinburgh, 1756).

[8] See Letter 21, n. 8, p. 34.

[9] See Letter 21, n. 11, p. 34.

[10] Probably William Strahan, a leading London printer.

[11] George William Coventry, sixth Earl of Coventry (?–1809). At this time he lived in Mayfair, and later in Piccadilly.

[12] Appius Claudius, Chief of the Decemvirs, leading character in Moncrieff's *Appius*.

[13] There is no such line spoken by Appius in the play as printed in 1755.

Decemvir exclaim 'Perdition sieze me but he has murdered her!', an Expression altogether similar and equivalent to 'he has killed her, God damn me if he has not!' Bob Smith, who happened to be in company with Crispe when he made this observation, chanced that same Evening to read his Virginia, and was so tickled with the Circumstance that he laughed all night sans Intermission. The ridiculous part of a Character never escapes Bob. I have nothing at present to entertain you with, and my head is confused, so that I must conclude with my Benediction. May the Lord have you in his protection! amen.

yours unaffectedly,
T: Smollett

Address: Not available. *Source:* MS. at NLS. *First Printing: TLS* (31 July 1943), by Henry W. Meikle.

Letter 23
To John Moore

Chelsea, April 16th, 1754

John,

The Bearer is my worthy friend Mr. Smith,[1] tutor to Lord Gairlies;[2] I cannot make you a more valuable present than that of his Acquaintance. Cherish it therefore and introduce him to Barclay,[3] Blackburn,[4] and all the honest fellows of your Town. He will improve upon you every day, and you will have reason to thank me for the opportunity of knowing him. I understand there are certain Prigs[5] of Glasgow who have endeavoured to do him ill offices by clandestine and malicious Insinuations. The Miscreants, whosoever they may be, are dissappointed, and God grant they may never have better Success in any of their Endeavours, for they must be sordid Knaves who could attempt to prejudice such an unblemished Character. Say not a word of this to Smith, whose deli-

[1] See Letter 3, n. 3, p. 5.
[2] See Letter 22, n. 6, p. 38.
[3] See Letter 2, n. 6, p. 1.
[4] Probably Andrew Blackburn, merchant in Glasgow. See *The Matriculation Albums of the University of Glasgow* (Glasgow, 1913), under 'Andreas Blackburn', who entered the university in 1733.
[5] Narrow-minded pedantic persons, Scottish clergymen included. Smollett's friend, Dr. Alexander Carlyle, defined clerical prigs in 1763 as 'half-learned . . . ignorant of the world, narrow-minded, pedantic, and overbearing'. See Carlyle, 463.

cacy might be hurt in the Explanation; and let it not be mentioned to any other person untill matters be more ripe for a Discovery. I offer my Respects to your Mother and Sisters and am

Dear John, yours most faithfully,
T. Smollett

Address: To Mr. John Moore Surgeon in Glasgow. *Source:* MS. of PTS. *First Printing:* Noyes, 30.

Letter 24

To Dr. George Macaulay

Chelsea, Saturday, Novr. 16th, 1754

Dear Doctor,

As yet I have not received an Answer to my Letter from Scotland; as soon as it arrives, I shall communicate the Purport of it to you. I am extremely chagrined to find you in such an hampered situation, and my Mortification is redoubled when I reflect upon my being in some measure the Cause.[1] I hoped that cursed ship from the East Indies[2] would have arrived before this time, and brought some good news; but every thing has of late thwarted my Schemes and Expectations, and therefore I cannot help dreading a Repulse from Scotland[3] also. Had I credit enough to borrow the money in London, you should not be without it a day longer, even though I should pay 50 per Cent for the Loan; but, believe me, I should find it difficult to raise half the sum in England, even to save me from a Jail. Never was I so much harrassed with Duns as now; a Persecution which I owe to the Detention of that Remittance from Jamaica, which I have expected every day since last Christmas, upon the Faith of Promises sent from time to time. I am, with great sincerity, gratitude, and affection,

Dr. Sir,
Yours intirely,
T. Smollett

Address: To Dr. Macaulay Poland Street. *Source:* MS. not located. *First Printing:* Anderson, 176–7.

[1] Smollett borrowed money repeatedly from his generous friend, Dr. George Macaulay.

[2] Nothing is known about Smollett's possible source of income in the East Indies.

[3] This means the possible refusal of Smollett's brother-in-law, Alexander Telfer, or someone else in Scotland to lend Smollett money at this time.

Letter 25

To Dr. George Macaulay

Chelsea, Dec. 11, 1754

Dear Sir,

Upon my honour, I have not had the least answer to the letter I wrote to Scotland, nor has one farthing arrived from Jamaica,[1] circumstances which fill me with astonishment and mortification. And what increases my wonder is to hear that Mr. Telfer[2] is, or was lately, at Edinburgh. I would still hope that a favourable answer might be received from that country; otherwise, methinks they would have signified their refusal, as I pressed the thing in such strong terms. For my own part, I never was reduced to such a dilemma as I am now brought into; for I have promised to pay away tradesmens' bills, to a considerable amount, by Christmas; and my credit absolutely depends upon my punctuality. Nay, I am put to very great straits for present subsistence as I have done nothing all the last summer but worked upon Don Quixotte, for which I was paid five years ago.[3] If my joint security could be of any service in raising a sum of money until matters shall clear up, I would cheerfully pay the premium for insuring my life;[4] and as my friends are good, I think it would not be a bad expedient. In short, I am so distracted with my difficulties that I cannot form any other feasible scheme for the present emergency, and I wish you would consider how it might be altered or improved. I am, with great affection, gratitude, and regard,

Yours etc.,
T^s Smollett

I was last night robbed of my watch and money in the stage coach between this and London,[5] and am just going to town to inquire about the robber.

Address: Not available. *Source:* MS. not located. *First Printing: Scots Magazine* (May 1804). The above text follows that in Anderson, 177.

---

[1] The income from Mrs. Smollett's property in Jamaica was often very late in reaching England.

[2] Smollett's brother-in-law.

[3] For details on Smollett's prolonged work in translating *Don Quixote* see Knapp, 44, 105–6, 163–5.

[4] Nothing is known about Smollett's possible life-insurance.

[5] Noyes, 142.

Letter 26

To John Moore

Chelsea, Decr. 11, 1755

Dear Sir,

I never repined so much at my own want of Importance as at this Conjuncture when you have Occasion for the Interest of your Friends; and it is with great Mortification I now assure you that I have no sort of Connexion with the Great Man who is to decide between you and your Competitor.[1] Far from being used to the Great, as you seem to imagine, I have neither Interest nor acquaintance with any Person whose Countenance or Favour could be of advantage to myself or my friends. I live in the shade of obscurity, neglecting and neglected, and spend my vacant hours among a Set of honest, phlegmatic Englishmen whom I cultivate for their Integrity of Heart and Simplicity of Manners. I have not spoke to a Nobleman for some years; and those I once had the Honour of knowing were either such as had little Interest of their own, or very little Consideration for me.

I am heartily sorry to find your Cause is so slenderly supported with the Duke of Argyle[2] because, without his Concurrence or rather his creative Word, I believe no Professorship can be filled up. Merit is altogether out of the Question. Every thing here as well as in your Country is carried by Cabal; and in Scotland, the Cabal of the Campbells will always preponderate. The Time is fast approaching when all the Lands, all the Places of Honour, Power and Profit will be in the possession of that worthy Clan. Then you may exclaim *non Numinis sed Campbellorum omnia plena!*[3]

Present my best wishes to Mrs. Moore and all your family; and be assured (if such a Declaration can be of any Consequence to a man whom I cannot serve in any thing essential) that I am with equal Truth and affection,

Dear Sir, Your very humble Servt.,
Tʼ Smollett

If you are acquainted with Capt. Walter Graham of Kilmannan,[4] make my Compts. to him and tell him that I intend one of these days to answer his Letter, with which I was favoured some weeks

---

[1] Dr. John Moore was perhaps hoping for a position at Glasgow University.

[2] Archibald Campbell, third Duke of Argyll.

[3] Translated this means: all things are full, not of divine power, but of Campbells.

[4] Unidentified.

ago. I should likewise be glad to be remembered to Bob Barclay,[1] Andrew Blackburn,[2] Will Wood,[3] and the rest of my Glasgow friends.

Address: Not available. *Source:* MS. owned by PTS. *First Printing:* In part by Irving, 18–19. The text in Noyes, 33–4, lacks the postscript.

Letter 27

To ? James Smollett, Esq., of Bonhill[4]

Chelsea, March 9th, 1756

Dear Sir,

Your very kind Letter afforded me real Pleasure because it breathes genuine Friendship and Sincerity. Such Language of the Heart I prefer to all the Frippery of Eloquence, to all the Bribes of Ostentation. The Circumstances of our Cousin Theophilus[5] is to me amazing, and resembles the suggestion of a Dream. I feel a strange Curiosity to see the man. What says Mrs. Bethune[6] and the females of our Family? Considering the low Ebb to which we are reduced, this is a sort of acquisition to the Name. I begin to think we were originally Malet or Molet and came from Normandy with the Conqueror. He had followers of both names, and they settled in the north. William Malet[7] was governour of York and a very gallant officer. The S. may have shifted its place from the End of the Prenomen to the Beginning of the Surname.[8] There is a Norman who keeps a public House in the skirts of Chelsea, of the name of Jonas Mollet. I have by me an old Diploma signed at Caen about an hundred years ago, SMALET antiquior Scholae Medicinalis Magister. I should be very glad to know if you have any anecdotes of our little Family; I have been told they were freeholders in Dumbarton four hundred years ago.[9] By the bye I find Dumbarton was once the Capital of the Kingdom of Arecluyd inhabited by Britons or Cumbrians, whence it[s] name of Dunbritton; that this

[1] See Letter 2, n. 6, p. 1. [2] See Letter 23, n. 4, p. 39. [3] See Letter 2, n. 1, p. 3.
[4] The probable recipient of this letter, Smollett's cousin, was a Commissary of Edinburgh, and Sheriff-Depute of Dumbartonshire, who purchased Cameron House on Loch Lomond in 1763. He was host to Boswell and Johnson in 1773. For other Smolletts having the Christian name of James, see Noyes, 144.
[5] Unidentified. [6] See Letter 18, n. 2, p. 29.
[7] For an account of William Mallet (?–1071) see *DNB*.
[8] The origin of Smollett's family name remains uncertain. For conjectures, see Noyes, 145–6.
[9] Joseph Irving, in his Bonhill Parish Genealogies, referred to John Smollett, Baillie of Dumbarton in 1516. See Irving (1860), 336.

Kingdom extended westerly to the Extremity of Cunningham or the Cumera Islands in the mouth of the Clyde; that it was bounded by the Forth on one Side and the irish Channel on the other. The greatest part of Dumbarton has been destroyed by an Inundation. I myself when a Boy have felt the Stones of the Pavement under water between what is called the College and the Town's End. I think I remember to have seen the Ruins of old Stone Houses on the other side of the Sands, and on your Ground at the Stony flat there are many Remains of Druid Worshipping Places. I am persuaded that an antiquarian would find much entertainment about Dumbarton, and even some noble monuments of roman Antiquity; for there was a stationary Camp within three miles of the Place, at Kilpatrick, for the Guard of the Wall built by Lollius Urbieus in the Reign of Antoninus,[1] commonly called Graeme's Dyke, which Buchannan ignorantly confounds with the wall built by Severus from the Esk to the Tyne in the North of England; and as the Britons of Arecluyd were under the roman Protection, they must have entertained an intimate Intercourse, and without doubt the Roman Generals and officers of Rank lived at Dunbritton. You will think this is a strange Rhapsody, but to me the subject is interesting. I have had occasion lately to inquire into the antiquities of our Country. I find the Scots came from Ireland but yesterday, in comparison with the antiquity of the Caledonians and Britons of Arecluyd. I would fain derive myself from these last, but whether antient Scot, Briton or Norman, I certainly am with equal affection and Esteem, Dr. Sir,

Your very humble Servt.,
T⁹ Smollett

My wife presents her best wishes for Mrs. Smollett and you. I hope mine will also be acceptable.

Address: Not available. *Source:* MS. owned by PTS. *First Printing:* Noyes, 35–7. Facsimile in Irving (1860), opposite p. 334.

Letter 28

To Dr. George Macaulay

Chelsea, April 6, 1756
Dear Doctor,

I have been last week threatened with writs of arrest, and some

[1] For the Roman wall in this area, see Irving, *op. cit.*, 8–10. See also Smollett's *The Present State of All Nations*, 8 vols. (London, 1768–9), ii, 97.

tradesmen in Chelsea have been so clamorous that I actually promised to pay them in the beginning of this week. I had recourse to Mr. Rivington,[1] who happens to be out of cash, in consequence of breaking up partnership with his brother. My proposal was that he should advance 100 l. which I would pay at the rate of four guineas per week, deducted from the History;[2] and at that rate I should have liquidated the debt in about three-and-twenty weeks. He had no sort of objection to the scheme, and agrees to join with me in security for the money if it can be borrowed for six months or longer. As he is a sufficient man, and this disgrace hovers over my imagination so as that I shall be rendered incapable of prosecuting my scheme,[3] I have recourse to your advice and assistance. If you can command the sum, the deduction of four guineas a week shall be made into your own hands; and even after the payment of that sum I shall go on towards a general clearance until I am enabled to discuss[4] the rest of my debt to you by remittances from the West or East Indies. This proposed scheme of liquidation, added to the unquestionable security of Mr. Rivington, and the consideration of my condition, will, I doubt not, prevail upon you to exert yourself in behalf of, dear Sir, yours, etc.,

[T.̤ Smollett]

Address: Not available. *Source:* MS. not located. *First Printing:* Anderson, 178.

Letter 29

To John Moore

Chelsea, Augt. 3, 1756

Dear Sir,

I am sorry to find that the young Gentleman you recommended to my acquaintance had the Trouble of calling at my House without

[1] John Rivington (1740–92), publisher and bookseller, who because of the alleged unethical business methods of his brother and partner, James Rivington, severed relations with him in 1756. See *A Dictionary of Printers and Booksellers* (Oxford University Press, 1932), 214; J. A. Cochrane, *Dr. Johnson's Printer, The Life of William Strahan* (London, 1964), *passim*; and Septimus Rivington, *The Publishing House of Rivington* (London, 1919).

[2] Smollett's *Complete History of England* was being printed for James Rivington and James Fletcher when Smollett wrote this letter.

[3] This may refer to Smollett's unsuccessful project for an academy of belles-lettres (Knapp, 167–8, and Letter 29).

[4] Shake off, remove.

seeing me. I was so liable to Intrusion from the situation of my House and the number of my friends that I found it absolutely necessary to give my servant[1] a general order to deny me to all those with whom I had no express Business; but, if Mr. Dougal[2] had left his name or mentioned your's, I should have had the Pleasure of seeing him. You may assure yourself that every Person whom you introduce shall always be welcome to my best offices, which, God knows, are very inconsiderable.

By your asking if I am engaged in any new Performance, and, immediately after, mentioning the Critical Review, I conclude you have been told I am concerned in that work. Your information has been true. It is a small Branch of an extensive Plan which I last year projected for a sort of Academy of the belles Lettres,[3] a Scheme which will one day, I hope, be put in Execution to its utmost Extent. In the meantime the Critical Review is conducted by four Gentlemen of approved abilities,[4] and meets with a very favourable Reception.[5]

Tho' I never dabble in Politics, I cannot help saying that there seems to have been no Treachery in delivering up St Philip's fort,[6] nor even in the scandalous affair with the french fleet, which was owing to the personal Timidity of our admiral,[7] who is at present

---

[1] Alexander Tolloush. (Knapp, 74.)

[2] Probably J. Dougall of Easter House, near Glasgow, and a member of the Hodge-Podge Club, Glasgow. For Dr. John Moore's reference to him in light verse, see Dr. John Strang's *Glasgow and its Clubs* (1856), 50.

[3] Unfortunately, nothing specific is known about this interesting plan projected by Smollett in 1755.

[4] There have been speculations concerning the names of these four gentlemen, both including and excluding Smollett himself.(Noyes, 148–50, and Knapp, 172–7.) About 1957, Mr. Derek Roper discovered in the library of the University of Oregon copies of the first two volumes of the *Critical Review* with manuscript annotations indicating the names of the reviewers. See Derek Roper, 'Tobias Smollett and the Founders of his "Review"', *The Call Number* (Eugene, Oregon), xix (1957), 4–9, and also Derek Roper, 'Smollett's "Four Gentlemen"': the First Contributors to the *Critical Review*', *RES*, (Feb. 1957), 38–44. In these volumes the names indicated in marginal manuscript are Dr. Thomas Francklin, Professor of Greek at Oxford; Samuel Derrick; Dr. John Armstrong; and Smollett himself, to whom in the first volume alone some seventy reviews are ascribed. For lost sets of the *Critical Review*, some of them probably annotated, see Knapp, 173, n. 7.

[5] In the early years of the *Critical Review* it was frequently attacked, Smollett being the chief target. It is doubtful whether after 1756 Smollett always regarded its reception as 'very favourable'.

[6] In June 1756, this fort, located on the island of Minorca in the Mediterranean, was captured by the French.

[7] Admiral John Byng, who was executed in 1757. For Smollett's later opinion of him see his *Continuation of the Complete History of England*, i, 470–80.

the object of the public Detestation. Indeed, the People seem to be in a ferment, and there are not wanting rascally Incendiaries to inflame their Discontent so that in a populace less phlegmatic the Consequences would in all probability be very mischievous.

Make my kind Compliments to Dr. Stevenson,[1] Messrs. Barclay,[2] Blackburn,[3] Fogo,[4] and all my Glasgow friends, and allow me to be unalterably

Dr John, your very affectionate humble servt.,

T: Smollett

If Lieutenant William Wood[5] be in Glasgow, give my service to him, and tell him I am infinitely obliged to him for the pains he took in the affair which he knows. I think I wrote to him on this subject, and should be glad to know if my memory serves me right as to that Particular. I must likewise desire you will present my best Respects to your Mother, and Mrs. Moor, who, I hope, has brought you all the Comforts of Wedlock.

Address: Not available. *Source:* MS. of PTS. *First Printing:* In part by Irving, 19. The text in Noyes (38–40) lacks the postscript.

Letter 30

To Samuel Richardson[6]

Chelsea, Augt. 10, 1756

Sir,

I was extremely concerned to find myself suspected of a silly, mean Insinuation against Mr. Richardson's Writings, which appeared some time ago in the Critical Review,[7] and I desired my friend Mr. Millar[8] to assure you in my name that it was inserted

[1] Dr. Alexander Stevenson. He obtained his M.D. at the University of Glasgow in 1749 and became Professor of Medicine there in 1766.

[2] See Letter 2, n. 6, p. 1.   [3] See Letter 23, n. 4, p. 39.   [4] Dr. Moore's cousin.

[5] Probably not the Will Wood referred to by Smollett in Letter 2.

[6] Samuel Richardson (1689–1761), the prominent novelist, printer, publisher, and Master of the Stationers' Company in 1754.

[7] Smollett had in mind, perhaps, a short digressive attack on Richardson's prolixity in a review of a novel, *The Supposed Daughter*, in the *Critical Review*, i (Apr. 1756), 261: 'This at least we can say in his favour . . . his relations are told with brevity; and had the writer of *Sir Charles Grandison* . . . worked upon his materials, he would easily have swelled them into twenty folio volumes.' In the next issue of the *Critical Review*, i (May 1756), 315, there was a short compliment to Richardson, perhaps inserted at Smollett's request.

[8] See Letter 21, n. 1, p. 35.

(47)

without my privity or Concurrence. Tho' you received his Explanation with your usual Candour, I think it my Duty to corroborate what he has said in my Vindication by protesting in the most solemn Manner that I never once mentioned Mr. Richardson's name with disrespect, nor ever reflected upon him[1] or his writings by the most distant hint or allusion; and that it is impossible I should ever mention him either as a writer or a man without Expressions of admiration and applause. I am not much addicted to Compliment; but I think Such an Acknowledgement is no more than a piece of Justice due to that amiable Benevolence, sublime morality and surprizing Intimacy with the human Heart, which must ever be the objects of Veneration among People of good Sense and Integrity.[2] I am very much obliged to you for your judicious Remarks on the Plan of my History,[3] and shall be proud of your advice on any future Occasion; in the meantime I beg leave to profess myself with the most perfect Esteem.

Sir, your very humble Servt.,
T! Smollett

Address: Not available. *Source:* MS. in HSP. On the same MS. is Richardson's reply. *First Printing: Monthly Magazine*, vol. xlviii (1819), 326.

Letter 31

To Dr. George Macaulay

Chelsea, September 10, 1756

Dear Doctor,

The fund which I appropriated for the payment of that note I have been obliged to pay on another score.[4] I would willingly have concealed the affair from your knowledge, but it must now come out in my own justification. About two years ago, Captain

[1] Nor ever cast reproach or blame upon him.

[2] In his *Continuation of the Complete History of England*, iv (1761), 128, Smollett's appraisal of Richardson runs as follows: 'The laudable aim of inlisting the passions on the side of virtue, was successfully pursued by Richardson, in his Pamela, Clarissa, and Grandison; a species of writing equally new and extraordinary, where, mingled with much superfluity and impertinence, [i.e. irrelevance] we find a sublime system of ethics, an amazing knowledge, and command of the human nature.'

[3] For Smollett's 'Plan of The Complete History of England', see vol. i of that work (London, 1757) on pages preceding the 'Errata in volume I'. The 'Plan' is not an outline but a comprehensive statement of the nature of the whole work.

[4] A sum recorded to a customer's debt. A bill.

To Dr. George Macaulay, 10 September 1756

Crawfurd[1] had a law-suit with his servant about wages, &c. He was bailed by Dr. Macculloch[2] and me. He left the suit to the care of Adam Gordon,[3] and went to Scotland. Gordon neglected the suit, and judgment being given against the defendant, we, his bail, were obliged to pay damages, costs, &c. to the amount of 95 l. I drew upon Crawfurd for the money: aftre [*sic*] some shuffling, he agreed to accept of a bill, payable in eight months. The bill was sent down for him for his acceptance; he never answered the letter. We have instituted a process against him, and were forced to pay the bill, with costs, on its being returned protested. This is the truth, and nothing but the truth. So help me God! The money will be recovered, as he is a man of fortune. In the meantime, I will endeavour to borrow as much as will take up Hamilton's note.[4] If I cannot and they should prove troublesome, I must remove to some corner where I may work without being distracted and distressed, for here I can do nothing. I have done very little for these two months past, and am engaged to finish the History[5] by Christmas, so that you may guess my situation. When I sat down to this work I was harrassed by duns; I have paid above one hundred pounds of debts, which I could no longer put off, and maintained my family. I have since paid £120 to different tradesmen from a small remittance which we lately received. I could not have disposed of that money otherwise without being disgraced. We have granted ample powers to Tom Bontein[6] to sell our Negroes in the West Indies. He has promised, upon honour, to remit what is already due (amounting to above £1000 sterling) with the first opportunity. We expect daily remittances from the Harvies,[7] and I am determined to make no use of what comes, except for the payment of debts, until the whole are liquidated. You have interposed so often with Mr. Maclean[8] that I am ashamed to mention any expedient of that sort. I have

[1] Captain John Walkinshaw Craufurd of Craufurdland (Alice Parker, 'Tobias Smollett and the Law', *Studies in Philology*, xxxix, (1942), 549; and Knapp, 'Early Scottish Attitudes toward Tobias Smollett', *Philological Quarterly*, xlv, Jan. 1966, 263.

[2] See Letter 13, n. 1, p. 20.

[3] Perhaps Lord Adam Gordon, M.P. for Aberdeenshire in 1754.

[4] Perhaps Archibald Hamilton, Senior, a prominent printer.

[5] *Complete History of England.*   [6] See Letter 13, n. 2, p. 19.

[7] Alexander and John Harvie were Smollett's attorneys in Kingston, Jamaica in 1756 (Knapp, 219, n. 99).

[8] Smollett referred to one Mr. McLean (or MacLeane) in several letters, including Letter 49 (Jan. 6, 1758), which Noyes misdated 1750. See Noyes, 119, where he suggested that it was 'barely possible' that this McLean was Laughlin MacLeane, a wealthy friend of John Wilkes. That Smollett knew him seems quite likely because a friend of Lauchlin McLean was Hugh Macaulay (later Macaulay-Boyd) the nephew of Dr. George Macaulay (James N. M. Maclean's *Reward is Secondary . . .* (London, 1963), 214–15).

some irons in the fire for borrowing a little money to satisfy those gentlemen. I have desired my agent to offer any premium rather than be disappointed, and I will let you know the result of his endeavours. I am, as ever, dear Doctor, your most affectionate and much obliged humble servant, etc.,

[T.^{s} Smollett]

Address: Not available. *Source:* MS. not located. *First Printing:* Anderson, 178–9.

Letter 32
To Dr. Macaulay

Chelsea, Novr. 24, 1756

Dr. Dr.,

I think I may now with Confidence beg your Interposition with Mr. Maclane[1] about Hamilton's[2] Note, as the Farce[3] which is coming on immediately will undoubtedly enable me to discharge that obligation. I just now recieved an Intimation[4] from him requiring immediate Payt. which is as much out of my power as the imperial Crown of England. I need say no more than that I am,

Dr. Sir,
Yours intirely,
T.^{s} Smollett

Address: To Dr. Macaulay at his House in Poland Street. *Source:* MS. of Mr. Robert H. Taylor. *First Printing:* Anderson, 179–80.

Letter 33
To William Huggins[5]

Chelsea, Decr. 7, 1756

Dear Sir,

I send my Spaniard[6] to return the Compliment I have recieved

[1] See Letter 31, n. 8, p. 49. [2] See Letter 31, n. 4, p. 49.
[3] *The Reprisal*, first staged 22 Jan. 1757 at the Theatre Royal in Drury Lane.
[4] Formal notification.
[5] William Huggins (1696–1761), whom Smollett visited at Headley Park, Hampshire. Huggins was the first Englishman to translate Dante's *Divine Comedy* (a translation never published, and since lost). His translation of Ariosto's *Orlando Furioso* was published in London in 1757. See Powell, 179.
[6] *The History and Adventures of the renowned Don Quixote*, 2 vols. (London, 1755). This translation was published in Feb. 1755.

by your Italian.[1] Cervantes was a warm Admirer of Ariosto, and therefore Don Quixote cannot be disagreable to a Lover of Orlando furioso. Though I do not pretend to compare my Prose with your Poetry, I beg you will accept of my Translation as a mark of that Perfect Esteem with which I have the Honour to be

Sir,

Your most obedt. humble servt.,

T: Smollett

Address: Not available. *Source:* MS. not located. *First Printing:* By Claude Jones in *MLN* (April, 1935), 242–3.

Letter 34
To Dr. Macaulay

Chelsea, Decr. 14, 1756

Dear Doctor,

I am again sollicited in behalf of that poor man Mr. Hamilton.[2] His account is settled to the satisfaction of every Body. He wants to go to Scotland, is starving in London, and in danger of being arrested for small Debts. He says if Mr. Maclean[3] will pay the money on the Attachment's being laid,[4] he will find Sureties for an Indemnification.[5] In that Case he cannot possibly be a Loser. I am really shocked at giving you so much trouble about myself and other miserable Suppliants, but this man makes me extremely unhappy; and I know you take pleasure in the Exercise of Benevolence. Besides, Mr. Milne[6] is his Creditor,[7] and at present in great Want of money for his Christmas Payments. He is likewise mine, and if this money can be procured for Mr. Hamilton, he will excuse me for the present. We must therefore once more have Recourse to your good offices. Mr. Garrick in a very civil Letter

[1] *Orlando Furioso by Lodovico Ariosto Translated from the Italian*, 2 vols. (London, 1757). William Huggins may have sent Smollett a copy of his translation, first published anonymously in 1755, or an advance copy of the edition published in 1757. In the beginning of a review, probably by Smollett, one reads the following: 'Though this work was printed before the *Critical Review* commenced, it did not appear in public till the year 1756, and therefore it falls properly under our cognizance.' (*Critical Review*, iii (May 1757), 385).

[2] Unidentified.

[3] See Letter 31, n. 8, p. 49.

[4] On the legal seizure's being imposed as a penalty.

[5] Pledges for payment.

[6] Unidentified. Possibly 'Mr. Miln, the merchant' of Letter 18.

[7] One to whom a debt is owing.

gave me to understand that it will be proper to defer the Representation of my Piece till after the Holidays.[1] I have inclosed a begging Card belonging to a Countryman of ours, one Forbes.[2] The man I know not, but the Prize is an Elegant Book. I am with glowing Gratitude and affection,

Dear Sir,
yours intirely,
T⦚ Smollett

I wish you could get an Article for the next number of the Review,[3] on painting, Statuary or Engraving. What do you think of the Bacchus?[4] Upon second Thoughts I have sent you two Cards. Perhaps Dr. Hunter[5] or Dr. Clephane[6] will take one.

Address: To Dr. Macaulay London. *Source:* MS. in NLS. *First Printing:* Anderson, 180, the date of this letter being misprinted there as 1759.

Letter 35

To David Garrick[7]

[*c.* January, 1757]

Sir,

Understanding from Mr. Derrick[8] that some officious people have circulated reports in my name with a view to prejudice me in your

---

[1] Smollett's *The Reprisal* was staged on 22 Jan. 1757.

[2] Unidentified.

[3] No such article appears in the *Critical Review* for Jan. or Feb. 1757.

[4] Unlocated.

[5] Dr. William Hunter (Letter 10, n. 2).

[6] Dr. John Clephane, F.R.S. (?–1758), a successful Scottish doctor who lived in Golden Square, and a very close friend of David Hume. See Ernest Campbell Mossner, *The Life of David Hume* (Nelson, 1954), *passim*. Clephane became a physician at St. George's Hospital in 1751.

[7] David Garrick (1717–79), the brilliant actor. Garrick permitted the unknown editor of Smollett's *Plays and Poems* (1777), to print this and several other letters received from Smollett. For a detailed account of the relationships between Garrick and Smollett, see Knapp, 'Smollett and Garrick', in *Elizabethan Studies and Other Essays in Honor of George F. Reynolds* (Boulder, Colorado, 1945), 233–43. See also Noyes, 156–8.

[8] Samuel Derrick (1724–69), later Master of Ceremonies at Bath. He produced a great variety of minor writings, including a volume of poems (1755), for which Smollett subscribed, and he probably contributed to the *Critical Review*. For his portrait, see the first volume of his two-volume work entitled *Letters Written from Liverpoole, Chester, Corke, The Lake of Killarney, Dublin, Tunbridge-Wells, Bath* (London, 1767). Numerous letters by and to Derrick are in the Victoria and Albert Museum, London.

opinion, I, in justice to myself, take the liberty to assure you that if any person accuses me of having spoken disrespectfully of Mr. Garrick, of having hinted that he solicited for my farce, or had interested views in bringing it up on the stage, he does me wrong, upon the word of a gentleman. The imputation is altogether false and malicious. Exclusive of other considerations, I could not be such an ideot [*sic*] to talk in that strain when my own interest so immediately required a different sort of conduct. Perhaps the same insidious methods have been taken to inflame former animosities, which, on my part, are forgotten and self-condemned. I must own you have acted in this affair of the farce with that candour, openness, and cordiality, which even mortify my pride while they lay me under the most sensible[1] obligation; and I shall not rest satisfied until I have an opportunity to convince Mr. Garrick that my gratitude is at least as warm as any other of my passions. Meanwhile I profess myself,

Sir,
Your humble Servant,
T. Smollett

Address: Not available. *Source:* MS. not located. *First Printing: Plays and Poems written by T. Smollett, M.D.* (London, 1777, vi–vii); in Noyes, 44.

Letter 36

To David Garrick

Chelsea, Feby. 4, 1757

Sir,

You will give me leave to express my warmest acknowledgements for the frank and generous manner in which your received my Performance,[2] and the friendly Care you have exerted in preparing it for the stage.[3] I am still more particularly obliged by your allotting the sixth Night for my Benefit, instead of the Ninth to which only I was intitled by the Custom of the Theatre, and your acting on my Night I consider as an additional Favour. To Crown all these Benefits, you will, I hope, order the Piece to be acted occasionally that it may have some Chance of being saved from

---

[1] Grateful.

[2] *The Reprisal: or, the Tars of Old England.*

[3] For Garrick's possible direction of the rehearsals of *The Reprisal*, see Knapp, 197.

(53)

Oblivion;[1] but, whether you shall think it proper to comply with this Request, or judge it convenient to let the Tars go to bottom, I shall ever retain the most gratefull Sense of your Friendship, and eagerly seize every opportunity of manifesting that sincerity with which I am,

Sir,

your most obliged, and obedt. Servt.,

T: Smollett

Should it ever lie in my way to serve Mr. Garrick, I hope he will command me without Reserve. He cannot do any thing that will more oblige his humble servant.

Address: Not available. *Source:* MS. of Mr. Robert H. Taylor. *First Printing:* By Knapp, in *Elizabethan Studies and Other Essays in Honor of George F. Reynolds* (Boulder, Colorado, 1945), 233–43.

Letter 37

To William Huggins[2]

Chelsea, Feby. 19, 1757

Dear Sir,

The Pleasure I received in reading your Friend's Performance[3] was equal to the Honour you have done me in submitting it to my Perusal. The Characters are in my opinion artfully contrasted and well sustained. The Fable is interesting and the Diction spirited, but indeed that stream must needs flow delicious which takes its origin from the Fountain of Ariosto. Why was old Scotia robbed of the Honour of the scene? Not but that I think the names are altered for the Better. Areodante, Genevra, and Polenessa are not such tragical appellations as Polydore, Isabella and Alphonso. I think the Catastrophe would have a fine Effect upon the English stage, but I would wish to have seen a tender Scene between Isabella and Polydore, which I imagine would interest the Audience still more in their behalf, and the better prepare it for the excessive Grief manifested by Isabella at the supposed Death of her Lover. Are not the two successive soliloquies by Isabella and Villario towards the End of the third act too long? Will not the audience observe that the Deception at the Balcony is a stratagem practised

---

[1] For later performances of *The Reprisal* see Knapp, 201–2.

[2] See Letter 33.

[3] A lost play, *Polydore*, written by Huggins himself. See Powell, 184.

in the Play of Much ado about Nothing? How comes Villario into the Forrest in the Beginning of the fourth act? In this act, there are three long soliloquies, two by Alphonso and one by Argio, which I could wish to see curtailed. There are likewise some Expressions which I think might be altered for the better in different scenes of the Performance. These are all the Animadversions I shall presume to make upon a Piece replete with Merit. If you desire that I should put it into the Hands of Mr. Garrick, I will immediately comply with your Request, though I apprehend it as altogether impracticable to exhibit it this Season, which is already almost exhausted. Besides, my Interest with Mr. Garrick is so very low that I believe it would be much better received from any other Hand than mine.[1] I congratulate you upon the Proficiency you have made in the Spanish. I have read part of your Translation of Ariosto with equal Pleasure and Surprise, and am with inviolable Esteem,

Dear Sir,
Your most obliged humble Servt.,
T⁵ Smollett

Address: Not available. *Source:* MS. in HCSNJ. *First Printing:* By L. F. Powell in *MP,* xxxiv (1936), 184–5.

Letter 38

To William Huggins

London, April 13, 1757

Dear Sir,

I have just finished the third Volume of my History,[2] and am as sick of writing as ever an Alderman was of Turtle;[3] nevertheless, I have begun to read the Translation of Ariosto as a Critick, and perceive I shall make a very favourable Report of it to the Public.[4] I propose to have the Pleasure of seeing you about whitsuntide,[5]

[1] This appears to be an exaggerated statement (see Letter 35). Apparently Smollett did not wish to ask Garrick to read Huggins's play.

[2] The first three volumes of Smollett's *Complete History of England* were announced to be published shortly after he wrote this letter (see the *Public Advertiser* (11 Apr. 1757)). However, the exact time of their publication is not certain.

[3] Turtle Soup, or perhaps Mock Turtle, an imitation of turtle soup, made out of calf's head.

[4] What was probably Smollett's review appeared in the *Critical Review* for May 1757 (Letter 33, n. 1, p. 51).

[5] The days following Whit Sunday, i.e. the seventh Sunday after Easter.

and in the mean time hope you will excuse the abruptness of this address in consideration of the Labour I have lately undergone. I am with equal sincerity and affection,

Dear Sir,
Your much obliged Servt.,
T: Smollett

Address: Not available. *Source:* MS. in HCSNJ. *First Printing:* By L. F. Powell in *Eighteenth Century Studies*, Spiral Press, New York, 1970.

Letter 39

To Mr. James Rivington[1]

Chelsea, April 14, 1757

Dear Sir,

My neighbour John Lewis Bookbinder, alias Strap,[2] wants ten Copies of the History, which are bespoke by his Customers. The money will be returned as soon as he can deliver the Books, but he will expect to have them at Bookseller's Price. You will let him have them accordingly and oblige,

Dr. Sir,
Yours Sincerely,
T: Smollett

Address: To Mr. Jas. Rivington, Bookseller in Paternoster Row. *Source:* MS. in BM. *First Printing:* Noyes, 45. A facsimile in *The Works of Tobias Smollett with an Introduction by W. E. Henley* (1901), Frontispiece to vol. xii.

Letter 40

To John Moore

Chelsea, May 12, 1757

Dear Sir,

You will forgive me for not having answered your Letter sooner in consideration of the Hurry and Fatigue to which I have been exposed in bringing out my History of England. I sincerely rejoice in your success in Business, as well as in the Happiness you

---

[1] See Letter 28, n. 1, p. 45.　　　　[2] See Letter 19, n. 2, p. 31.

seem to enjoy amidst the Comforts of matrimony, and I beg leave
to make a Tender of my best wishes to Mrs. Moore as the source of
my friend's Happiness.[1] The little irishman[2] about whom you
express some Curiosity was my Amanuensis, and has been occasionally employed as a Trash reader for the Critical Review, but
you are not to number him among my Companions, nor indeed does
his Character deserve any further Discussion. The Bearer, Captain
Robert Man,[3] is my Neighbour in Chelsea, and I recommend him to
your friendship and acquaintance as a brave experienced officer and
an honest Tar in whom there is no Guile. He is appointed Captain of
the Porcupine sloop stationed in the Frith of Clyde, and being an
utter stranger in that part of the world, you must introduce him to
your and my friends at Glasgow, and asist him with your advice
and Directions. His Father was a Scotsman, and, I believe, a
native of your Town. My Friend Bob has been round the Globe
with Anson[4] and proved in fourteen or fifteen Sea Engagements,
during which he behaved with remarkable Gallantry; but his good
nature is equal to his Courage, and indeed he is the most inoffensive
man alive. If you want to know how I spend my Time in this
Retreat, he can satisfy you in that Particular, for he has been my
Club companion these seven long years.[5] Pray give my Compliments to Captain Graham[6] and tell him I had never once seen Dr.
Brisbane[7] 'till I met him accidentally about a month ago at Mr.
Barclay's[8] Lodgings. He seems to be in good Health and spirits,

[1] Moore had married in 1754 Miss Jean Simson, daughter of John Simson
(1688?–1740), Professor of Divinity at Glasgow. Moore's happiness at this time
was increased by the birth, on 9 Apr. 1757, of their second child, a son named
John. For this information I thank Prof. Henry L. Fulton.

[2] Possibly Samuel Derrick (Knapp, 178, n. 32).

[3] Capt. Robert Mann (d. 1762). See Noyes, 161. For details of Mann's naval
career and death, see Knapp, 115, n. 40. Smollett's friend is not to be confused
with another naval officer of the same name. See William Laird Clowes, *The
Royal Navy*, 5 vols. (London, 1898), iii, 308.

[4] Capt. Mann is not mentioned in George Anson's *A Voyage Round the
World* (1748). It is likely that Dr. Moore took Captain Mann to see Smollett's
cousin at Bonhill because in *Humphry Clinker* (Letter of Bramble, Cameron,
6 Sept.) it is stated that a captain of a man-of-war who had gone around the
globe with Anson exclaimed when he saw the family house at Bonhill in a
romantic glen: 'Juan Fernandez, by God.' In Anson's *Voyage* there are
numerous descriptions of the island of Juan Fernandez.

[5] Capt. Mann and Smollett may have been members of the Bowling Green
Society at Chelsea along with Dr. Alexander Reid.

[6] Unidentified.

[7] Probably Dr. John Brisbane, M.D., Edinburgh, 1750. He was physician to
the Middlesex Hospital, 1758–73. See Alexander Duncan, *Memorials of the
Faculty of Physicians and Surgeons of Glasgow 1599–1850*, (Glasgow, 1896),
[293].

[8] For Barclay, see Letter 2.

and that is all I know of the matter. Excuse haste and believe me to be,

Dear John,
Your affectionate friend and Servt.,
T.s Smollett

Address: To Mr. John Moore Surgeon in Glasgow. *Source:* MS. of PTS. *First Printing:* In part by Irving, 19; Noyes, 45–7.

Letter 41

To John Moore

Chelsea, June 4, 1757

Dear Sir,

I sympathize in your affliction[1] which I hope has neither been [so] immoderate nor so unmanly as to hinder you from acting the part of a Comforter to the Companion of your sorrows. I am pleased with the kind Expressions in which you mention my Dedication to Mr. Pitt,[2] who has treated me with that genuine Politeness[3] by which he is as much distinguished in private Life, as by his superior Talents in the service of his Country. I am afraid the History will not answer the Expectations that seem to be raised among my friends in Scotland. The fourth volume is now in the Press, and will (I believe) be published in three months, if no unforseen accident should intervene. You are right in your Conjecture with regard to the Criticism upon 'Douglas',[4] which I assure you I did not see untill it was in print. I did not write one article in that whole Number. By this time you have (I suppose) received my Letter by Capt. Mann[5] so that you will excuse me from writing at large on this occasion, especially as I am so fatigued with the unintermitting Labour of the Pen that I begin to loathe the sight of Paper. I am truly sorry for the Death of poor Dick,[6] for whom I

[1] Probably the loss of their infant son, John (Letter 40, n. 1, p. 57).

[2] See the beginning of vol. i of Smollett's *Complete History of England* for his dedication of this opus to William Pitt. It is an excellently written compliment, headed Chelsea, 25 Mar. 1757.

[3] For Pitt's appreciative note, see Noyes, 162. For the text of Pitt's note, written 15 May 1757, see Knapp, 'Smollett and the elder Pitt', *MLN*, lix (1944), 251.

[4] See the *Critical Review*, iii (Mar. 1757), 258–68, for the review of John Home's popular drama, *Douglas*.

[5] For Captain Robert Mann, see Letter 40, n. 3.

[6] Dr. Robert Dick, the younger, Professor of Natural Philosophy at the University of Glasgow, died 22 May 1757. See *Scots Magazine*, xix (May 1757), 278.

had a sincere Regard and warm affection. Present my Compliments and best wishes of Health and Happiness to Mrs. Moore. Let me be remembered to Dr. Stevenson,[1] and tell Mr. Barclay[2] I was much mortified to find he had left London without having crossed my Threshold. I understand he spent a genial Evening with some friends before he took his Departure. Though I am not a punctual Correspondent, I shall always be glad to hear from you, and it shall go hard but I will find means to acknowledge the Receipt of your favours. Meanwhile I profess myself your affectionate humble Servt.,

T:S Smollett

Address: Not available. *Source:* MS. of PTS. *First Printing:* Partly printed by Irving, 19–20; Noyes, 47–8.

Letter 42
To William Huggins

Chelsea, June 14, 1757

Dear Sir,

I thank you heartily for the Entertainment I have received from your Claudian.[3] I likewise acknowledge your obliging favour which this day came to my hands,[4] and I shall never forget your Friendship and Hospitality. I never once dreamed of translating Dante, a Task to which I am altogether unequal, a Task which ought to be reserved for the Translator of Orlando furioso.[5] Perhaps it might not run off like a Novel all at once, perhaps you are a little chagrined at the slowness of the English Ariosto,[6] but you will consider that it is not a Book for the mob of Readers. Yet the Character of it is established. The first Impression will drop away gradually, and in time it will become a standard Translation. This also might be the Fate of Dante, but I should be sorry such a Consideration should deter you from the Undertaking. You yourself observe you do not write in a Garret, nor are you a slave to Fame or Famine—*Macte virtute esto.*[7] You will not doubt that I should be proud of a Partner-

[1] For Dr. Stevenson, see Letter 29, n. 8.

[2] For Barclay, see Letter 2, n. 6, p. 1.

[3] Presumably a translation of some of the writing of the Latin poet, Claudius Claudianus, known as Claudian.

[4] Possibly some venison.   [5] Huggins.

[6] The slow sale of Huggins' translation of Ariosto's *Orlando Furioso.*

[7] Translated this means: 'Go on and prosper in well-doing.' This command is found, with slight variations, in the works of numerous Latin writers. See Horace, *Sermonum Liber Primus,* II, 31–2.

in
ship that would do me so much Honour; but I am so involved ~~with~~
[*sic*] the History of England,[1] and different Provinces of the
Universal History that I shall not for some years be able to engage
in any other work. I wonder you should make an apology for the
Prolixity of that which I always find too short and transistory,
but I hope you will not wonder that I should ask forgiveness for
my Brevity which is really owing to Hurry and Distraction. Were I
less perplexed, I should with pleasure expatiate on any subject
that might yield you Amusement, or tend to convince you of
that Esteem and affection with which I am,

Dear Sir,
your obliged humble servt.,
T: Smollett

I believe I shall trouble you with another Visit before the End of
Autumn. I beg leave to present my Compts. to good Mrs. Erskine,[2]
and to be kindly remembered to the two Divines.[3]

Address: Not available. *Source:* HCSNJ. *First Printing:* By L. F.
Powell in *Eighteenth Century Studies,* Spiral Press, New York, 1970.

Letter 43

To William Huggins

Chelsea, June 20, 1757
Dear Sir,

If I could ride as hard as you do Pegasus,[4] I should be at Headly
Park with a *Whoop* and at Chelsea with a *Hollow*.[5] What! are you
visited like Milton, in the night only,[6] or does your familiar[7] stand
always at your Elbow? You are quite the Muse's Mill that grinds all
weathers without Intermission. Your specimen I like as I do every

[1] Smollett was perhaps reading the proof of the fourth volume of his
Complete History of England. In Letter 41, he informed John Moore that it was
in the press.
[2] The Hon. Mrs. Annabella Erskine. See Powell, 192, n. 38.
[3] Unidentified.
[4] A winged steed on which poets ride in a symbolic sense.
[5] *Whoop* and *Hollow* were exclamations voiced in hunting.
[6] Smollett may have had in mind Milton's reference to his 'celestial Patron-
ess' who in her 'nightly visitation' dictated to him (*Paradise Lost,* ix, 21–2).
[7] *Familiar* means an attending familiar spirit, or demon. In the *OED*
Smollett's use of this word is cited. See the final paragraph of Ch. 38 in *Roderick
Random.*

thing that comes *ex tuâ Pharetrâ*.[1] I am dubious about some of the rhymes, such as *sight* and *quit*; but I have no objection to the Triplets if they are not too thick sown. Your scheme I shall be glad to know, as I suppose you have in your Eye some rich Mine from which [a] store of precious metal may be extracted. I thank you cordially for your Kindnesses, and wish it may be in my Power to make a suitable Return. There is no occasion for comparing your Claudian[2] with the Original. You know I read part of the Latin while you recited the Translation; but I have not yet examined it with that Care which I would bestow if you intended it immediately for the Press. Alas! I have nothing but the Fag End of a tedious day to employ in answering your Letter. You talk of the *Pistrinum*[3] or Cart's Tail; that is, according to the Spanish Proverb, no more than *panpintado*,[4] Cakes and Gingerbread to what I undergo. I have been groaning all day under the weight of Tindal,[5] Ralph,[6] Burnet,[7] Feuquieres,[8] Daniel,[9] Voltaire,[10] Burchet[11] &c., &c. and I have just spirits left to declare that I am,

Dear Sir,
Unalterably yours,
T: Smollett

Let me be respectfully remembred to Mrs. Erskine.[12] I have not yet seen my friend Monkhouse,[13] and I am nettled at his not coming to Chelsea. Franks[14] I have in plenty, so you need not afflict yourself on that Score.

Address: Not available. *Source:* HCSNJ. *First Printing:* By L. F. Powell in *Eighteenth Century Studies*, Spiral Press, New York, 1970.

[1] From your arrow-quiver.
[2] See Letter 42, n. 3, p. 59.
[3] Pounding mill.
[4] Painted bread or cake.
[5] Nicholas Tindal (1687–1774), historian.
[6] James Ralph (?–1762), a minor, versatile writer and author of a *History of England during the Reigns of King William, Queen Anne and King George I.*
[7] Probably Gilbert Burnet (1643–1714), Bishop of Salisbury and author of historical works.
[8] Antoine de Pas, Marquis of Feuquières (1648–1711), French military historian and critic.
[9] Samuel Daniel (1562–1619), English poet, dramatist and historian.
[10] Assumed name of François Marie Arout (1694–1778).
[11] Josiah Burchett (1666?–1746), author of naval histories.
[12] See Letter 42, n. 2, p. 60.
[13] See Powell, 179.
[14] Stationery bearing the signature of a person entitled to send letters post free. Who had given Smollett franks at this time is uncertain. In 1762 (Letter 86, Address) a frank from John Wilkes was used by Smollett.

Letter 44
To William Strahan

Chelsea, Monday Octr. 24, [? 1757]

Dear Sir,

As soon as I can spare a Day, I will let you know, and come to Town that you may not have the Trouble to come to the Country. I have perused the m.s. from Dr. R——y,[1] which is very sensible and correct, but I cannot well prepare it[2] for the Press without having the Synopsis and L——s's[3] Pamphlet, which I desire may be sent out, and I shall take care to return them in good Condition. I am obliged to you for your kind Interposition with Dr. Harvie.[4] It is a very hard case that I should be troubled with Duns for very small Sums when there are actually fifteen hundred pounds Sterling at the most moderate Computation due to us at Jamaica. I will not forget D——[5] and am always

your obliged humble servt. and
Sincere friend,
T.ˢ Smollett

Address: To Mr. W. Strahan, Printer in New Street. *Source:* MS. in PML. *First Printing:* Noyes, 48–9.

Letter 45
To ? Dr. George Macaulay

Chelsea, Novr. 5, 1757

Dear Sir,

After thanking you for all favours, I have only to add that I must infallibly find £50 in a few days in order to maintain myself in

[1] Dr. John Rutty (1698–1775), author of *A Methodical Synopsis of Mineral Waters* (London, 1757), and also of the remarkable *Spiritual Diary.* The former received favourable appraisals in the *Critical Review,* iv (1758), 121–30 and 242–56.

[2] For the works of Dr. Rutty which Smollett may have been preparing for publication, see Knapp, 207.

[3] Dr. Charles Lucas (1713–71), who violently attacked Dr. Rutty's medical book in a pamphlet, *An Analysis of Dr. Rutty's Methodical Synopsis,* which was ridiculed almost certainly by Smollett in the *Critical Review* iv (Aug. 1758), 160–2.

[4] Perhaps Dr. John Harvie of St. Ann's Parish, London, a beneficiary in the will of Dr. William Smellie, and the husband of Mrs. Smellie's niece (Knapp, 219, n. 99).

[5] Unidentified.

any sort of Tranquility. I do not see how I can hasten my agreement with Mr. Millar[1] any other way than by dispatching the work in which I am engaged, and that will certainly be finished by the end of the month.[2] I commit myself to your Protection, and am yours always,

T.^s Smollett

Address: Not available. *Source:* MS. not located. *First Printing:* Sale Catalogue of William Wright, 1899; see also Catalogue No. 354 of Myers & Co., London, 1948–9, item 200.

Letter 46
To ? Dr. Alexander Carlyle

Chelsea, Wednesday Evening [? 1758]

Dear Sir,

I was in hopes of hearing from you before this time. My affairs are very pressing. I shall be glad to see you at Forrest's[3] on Friday[4] evening at six o'clock. I am ever

Yours,
T.^s S^{tt}

Address: Not available. *Source:* MS. not located. See Noyes, 171. *First Printing:* Catalogue of William Wright, 1899.

Letter 47
To ?[5]

Chelsea, Wednesday noon [? November–December, 1757]

Dear Sir,

I have sent two Copies of P. P.[6] vol. 3.—Lady V——e's[7] story. You may compose from that which is incompleat in the other

---

[1] Andrew Millar, publisher.

[2] What work Smollett refers to is very uncertain. It was perhaps his *Complete History of England*, vol. iv.

[3] Forrest's Coffee-House in Charing Cross, opposite the Mews Gate. Dr. Alexander Carlyle dined there with Smollett in about Mar. 1758 (Carlyle, 347, 355 ff.).

[4] Printed *Tuesday* in Catalogue of William Wright, 1899. See Letter 45.

[5] The printer (or publisher) to whom Smollett sent this letter cannot be identified with certainty. It must have been one of the following publishers of the second edition of *Peregrine Pickle*: R. Baldwin, J. Richardson, D. Wilson, and T. Durham.

[6] *Peregrine Pickle.*   [7] Lady Vane.

Parts;[1] and if you think proper, you may prefix the two Letters in manuscript.[2] The remaining part of the 3d. volume you will find corrected in the other copy. The fourth shalt be done as soon as possible. I will take care of Mr. Johnston's Papers[3] and lick them up[4] in a very little time for their appearance. I wish you would send the proofsheets of Pickle to me to be corrected. As soon as I am at Leisure I intend to wait of [5] you, to complain of our friend Mr. Millar,[6] who, I understand, has done me ill offices about the History, and these in a very dishonourable manner; but of this more at meeting. He is mistaken if he thinks my being in his Debt authorizes him to do me Injuries with impunity. I shall not fail to insist upon Mr. Derrick's doing you Justice,[7] and I am very truly,

Dear Sir,

Your much obliged humble servt.,

T: Smollett

Address: Not available. *Source:* MS. at HU. *First Printing:* Noyes, 52.

Letter 48

To John Moore

Chelsea, Jany. 2, 1758

Dear Sir,

I deferred answering your kind Letter untill I should have finished my History[8] which is now compleated. I was agreably

---

[1] This complicated instruction means: you may print Lady Vane's story from the copy wherein only her story is revised (or corrected).

[2] These two letters were prefixed to the third volume of the second edition of *Peregrine Pickle*, published in 1758. The first, written as from Lady Vane, was addressed to 'Lord ———', and the 'Answer' was written to 'Madam'. After Smollett's 'Advertisement', printed at the beginning of the first volume, there is the following *Note*: 'The two letters relating to the Memoirs of a lady of quality, inserted at the beginning of the third volume, were sent to the editor by a person of honour.'

[3] Perhaps Dr. James Johnstone's *An Historical Dissertation concerning the Malignant Epidemical Fever of 1756; with an Account of the Malignant Diseases prevailing since the year 1752, in Kidderminster* (London, 1758). This one-shilling publication was reviewed in the *Monthly Review*, xviii (Mar. 1758), 244–7.

[4] Put into proper form.

[5] An obsolete expression meaning *call upon*. See *OED*.

[6] Andrew Millar, publisher.

[7] Samuel Derrick. See Letter 35, n. 8, p. 52. His relations to the recipient of this letter are unknown.

[8] The *Complete History of England* in four quarto volumes (1757–8).

surprised to hear that my work had met with any approbation at Glasgow, for it was not at all calculated for that meridian. The last Volume will, I doubt not, be severely censured by the west country whigs of Scotland; but, for you and other persons of sense and probity, I desire you will divest yourself of Prejudice, at least as much as you can, before you begin to peruse it, and consider well the Facts before you give Judgement. Whatever may be its defects, I protest before God I have, as far as in me lay, adhered to Truth without espousing any faction, though I own I sat down to write with a warm side to those principles in which I was educated. But in the Course of my Inquiries, the whig ministers and their abettors turned out such a Set of sordid Knaves that I could not help stigmatising some of them for their want of Integrity and Sentiment.[1]

I have for some time done very little in the Critical Review: The Remarks upon Home's Tragedy[2] I never saw untill they were in print, and as yet I have not read one Line of the Epigoniad.[3] I am told the work has merit, and am truly sorry that it should have been so roughly handled. Notwithstanding the Censures that have been so freely bestowed upon these and other Productions of our Country, the Authors of the C. Review have been insulted and abused as a *Scotch Tribunal*.[4] The Truth is there no Author so wretched but he will meet with Countenance in England if he attacks our Nation in any shape. You cannot conceive the Jealousy that prevails against us. Nevertheless, it is better to be envied than despised. I wish you and your family all Happiness, and am,

Dr. Sir,

Your affectionate humble servt.,

T<u>s</u> Smollett

Address: Not available. *Source:* MS. of PTS. *First Printing:* Partly printed by Moore, I, clxi. See Noyes, 166.

[1] For a helpful exposition of Smollett's change from being a Whig to a Tory, see Noyes, 166–7.

[2] *Douglas* (Letter 6, n. 6, p. 10).

[3] The *Epigoniad*, by the Scottish William Wilkie (1721–72), was unfavourably treated in the *Critical Review*, iv (July 1757), 27–35.

[4] Smollett referred here to Dr. John Shebbeare's *The Occasional Critic, or the Decrees of the Scotch Tribunal in the Critical Review Rejudged* . . . (London, [1757]). For an excellent account of the prolonged and violent conflict between Smollett and Shebbeare, see James R. Foster, 'Smollett's Pamphleteering Foe Shebbeare', *PMLA*, lvii (1942), 1053–1100.

Letter 49

To ?

Chelsea, Jany. 6, 1758

Dear Sir,

I wrote to Mr. Palmer of Ironmonger's Hall[1] that he should certainly hear from me this week, persuaded that I should have been able to transact that affair with Mr. M——,[2] so as to settle with Mr. Palmer; but I have been taken with a violent Cold which had like to have fallen upon my Lungs, and has confined me since Monday last. I have an appointment with Mr. M—— on Monday next; but in the mean time I should take it as a great favour if you would see Mr. Palmer, and tell him the Cause of my Delay, for I have received two different Messages from him, and one from Mr. McLean, importing that I am to expect no further Forbearance. I beg pardon for giving you this Trouble, and am,

Dear Sir,

your much obliged humble servt.,

Tˢ Smollett

I have a negotiation on foot for borrowing a Sum of money, in conjunction with another Gentleman; I do not believe it will succeed, but if any person comes to inquire my character of you, you will not be surprised.

Address: Not available. *Source:* MS. owned, at least until recently, by Oliver Barrett. *First Printing:* Noyes, 8–9, who misdated this letter 1750.

Letter 50

To Mr. [William] Strahan

Jany. 24, 1758

Dear Sir,

I have to day writt a Letter to Mr. Millar[3] on the subject you know. It is not couched in a begging stile, which I shall never use. I,

---

[1] Probably William Palmer, Clerk to the Worshipful Company of Ironmongers, who died 24 Oct. 1764. For his obituary, see *Gentleman's Magazine*, xxxiv, 499. In his will he bequeathed his property to his sisters, Barbara and Mary, and to his cousin, John Dyer, Linen Draper of London.

[2] Possibly the Mr. McLean mentioned towards the end of this letter. For McLean, see Letter 31, n. 8, p. 49.

[3] Andrew Millar, publisher (Letter 21, n. 1, p. 35).

nevertheless, am afraid he will decline my Proposal; and therefore I hope you will second it, in case he should ask your Advice, which in all probability he will. I am the more anxious on this Score, as a Refusal from him will oblige me to take certain Measures which, perhaps, he may dislike in the Sequel; for you know the money must be had, and that speedily; and I am not at all disposed to trouble Mr. Telfer,[1] whose friendship is too valuable to be risqued without an absolute necessity.

I am very truly,

Dr. Sir,

Your obliged humble servt.,

T! Smollett

Address: To Mr. Strahan. *Source:* MS. in PML. *First Printing:* Noyes, 9–10, who misdated this letter 1750.

Letter 51
To William Huggins

Chelsea, Feby. 17, 1758

Dear Sir,

I am much obliged to you for your kind Intention with Regard to Claudian,[2] as indeed I have reason to be for many other Favours which shall not be forgotten. But with respect to the proposal, I cannot help differing in opinion from my good friend. The Dedicatee,[3] as you are pleased to call him, has given me no ~~Reason~~ [*sic*] opening to present him with that or any other Compliment. Indeed, he is too much engaged in affairs of much greater Consequence for me to expect the least Notice or attention. Besides, it is not at all improbable that he dislikes the Execution of my Work. I declare I know nothing to the contrary. How far our friend Hamilton[4] might find his account in printing the Piece I cannot judge. This I know, that Poetry, at present, seems to be quite out of fashion. There is a compleat Translation of Claudian by Hughes,[5] and, as I am told, well executed, now lying as Lumber in a Bookseller's

[1] Probably Alexander Telfer of Symington, Smollett's brother-in-law (Letter 18).

[2] Presumably what Huggins had translated from the Latin Poet, Claudius Claudianus.

[3] Presumably William Pitt, to whom Smollett dedicated his *Complete History of England.*

[4] Probably Archibald Hamilton, Senior, printer of the *Critical Review.* (Knapp, Appendix D, and *passim.*)

[5] Jabez Hughes (1685–1731).

Warehouse. Shall I venture to drop a Hint of advice? Suppose our friend should publish it in his own Name, inscribed to Mr. Pitt.[1] Such a Compliment from a Country Gentleman who could not be suspected of an Author's interested[2] Views must meet with a favourable reception. This Consideration would even attract the notice of the Publick and give the Piece a fair chance for being read. But this I submit to your better Judgement. Please let my compts. be offered to Mrs. Erskine,[3] and allow me to be with equal Esteem and affection,

Dear Sir,

Your much obliged humble Servt.,

Ts. Smollett

Address: Not available. *Source:* HCSNJ. *First Printing:* By L. F. Powell in *Eighteenth Century Studies*, Spiral Press, New York, 1970.

Letter 52

To William Strahan

Chelsea, June 24, 1758

Dr. Sir,

Recieve inclosed a note for £50. In a few days I shall be with you. I have recieved good news from the East Indies[4] and am always yours,

Ts. Smollett

Address: To Mr. Wm. Strahan Printer in New Street by Fetter lane. *Source:* MHS. *First Printing:* Knapp, 208.

Letter 53

To William Huggins

Chelsea, July 2d, 1758

Dear Sir,

I think myself very much obliged to any Person who will take the Trouble to point out any Errors or Mistakes I may have committed

[1] It seems as if Huggins may have suggested that his translation of a portion of Claudian be published with Smollett's name as well as his own on the title-page, and that Smollett dedicate it to William Pitt in order to increase its sale.

[2] Selfish, or self-seeking in a financial sense.

[3] See Letter 42, n. 2, p. 60.

[4] Nothing is known about Smollett's income from the East Indies.

To William Huggins, 2 July 1758

in writing the History of England. I can safely say I had no other
view in the Execution of that work than historical Truth, which I
have displayed on all occasions to the best of my Knowledge
without Fear or affection.[1] I have kept myself independent of all
Connexions which might have affected the Candour of my Intention. I have flattered no Individual; I have cultivated no Party. I
look upon the Historian who espouses a Faction, who strains
Incidents or willfully suppresses any Circumstances of Importance
that may tend to the Information of the Reader, as the worst of
Prostitutes. I pique myself upon being the only Historian of this
Country who has had Honesty, Temper and Courage enough to be
wholly impartial and disinterested.[2] I may be allowed to speak so
far in my own Commendation, considering how I have been treated
in public and private by Envy, Malice and Ingratitude. When I
said impartial, I ought to have excepted the Infirmities of human
Nature in which I own myself involved. I have such a natural
Horrour of Cruelty that I cannot without uncommon Warmth
relate any Instance of Inhumanity. What I have said of Bambridge[3] I learned from the Journals of the House of Commons,[4] in
which I found such a Detail of Cruelties exercised upon Sir Wm.
Rich, Jacob Mendes Solas, Capt. John Mackpheadris, Robert
Castell, and Capt. David Sinclair, as excited the strongest Emotions
of Horrour, Pity, and Indignation. Now, my good Sir, I always
thought that in recounting matters of Fact an Historian could not
have Recourse to better Authority than the Journals of the House
of Commons, which are indeed, public Records authenticated by
the Sanction of the Legislature. What private Motives might have
influenced the Committee in giving their Report I know not, ~~but~~
and
[sic] shall be glad of any Information on the Subject. But I can
hardly think the Proto-corrupter, as you are pleased to call him,

[1] Excessive political or national partisanship.

[2] Smollett repeatedly asserted his impartiality, not only as an historian, but
also as a writer of reviews for the *Critical Review*. See his letter to Dr. John
Moore (Letter 48), and the 'Plan' of his *History of England* in the first volume of
that work. One statement, by C. H. Timperley, that Smollett offered to be
partial in writing his *History* is ridiculous (Knapp, 194, n. 103).

[3] For Smollett's account of the cruelty of Bambridge, the warden of Fleet
Prison in about 1729, see *The Complete History of England*, vol. iv (1758), 527–8.
In this same account an earlier warden of Fleet Prison, John Huggins, the
father of Smollett's friend, William Huggins, was also shown to be guilty of
extreme cruelties. Reading this account in Smollett's *History* must have em-
barrassed William Huggins, whose natural challenge of its accuracy led
Smollett to write this letter. But Huggins maintained his cordial friendship
with Smollett. The statements in Smollett's *History* are found in Powell, 186–7.

[4] See *Journals of the House of Commons*, XXI, 237, 247, 282. For Smollett's
use of these journals see L. F. Powell, *op. cit.*, 187, n. 26.

had any Connexion with the Committee, the Chairman of which was then at Variance with the Ministry. I congratulate you on your having finished the Translation of Ariosto,[1] and am with perfect Esteem,

Dear Sir,
Your affect. humble Servt.,
T⁚ Smollett

Address: Not available. *Source:* MS. at HCSNJ. *First Printing:* By L. F. Powell in *MP*, xxxiv (1936), 185–6.

Letter 54

To William Huggins

Chelsea, July 24, 1758

Dear Sir,

I was favoured with both your Letters in due Course, which I acknowledge as further Instances of your Friendship and generosity. When I conversed with Mr. Boult[2] at Farnham,[3] I had a young Physician in my Eye, whom I would have ventured to recommend to your Countenance[4] and Protection. But I now find he is otherwise engaged, and I, at present, know no other Person duly qualified who wants a Settlement in the Country. I am, nevertheless, eternally obliged to Mr. Huggins for the warmth and Kindness with which he expressed himself on this Subject. As to what concerns Martinelli,[5] I will frankly give my opinion. If he foresees any advantage to himself in closing with your proposals, he will doubtless embrace them, and perhaps cheat you into the Bargain. If he is an associate of Baretti,[6] I think it will be neither for your Reputa-

[1] In 1759 Huggins published a new translation of some cantos of *Orlando Furioso*, entitled *Part of Orlando furioso*. See *Boswell's Life of Johnson . . .*, revised by L. F. Powell, iv (1934), 475.

[2] Unidentified.

[3] Farnham, Surrey. Smollett would have passed through Farnham on his trips to see Huggins in Headley Park, Hampshire, near Wallop, located north of Stockbridge.

[4] Support.

[5] Vincenzio Martinelli (1702–85), author of *Istoria Critica della Vita Civile* (London, 1752), reviewed in the *Monthly Review*, vii, 143–55; and *Lettere Familiari e Critiche* (London, 1758), reviewed unfavourably in the *Critical Review*, v (Feb. 1758), 144–7. Another work is his *Istoria d'Inghilterra*, 3 vols. (London, 1770–3).

[6] Giuseppe Marc' Antonio Baretti (1719–89), Italian writer and lexicographer, who first came to England in 1751. He was a violent, complex character, but praised by Sir Joshua Reynolds, Edmund Burke, Garrick,

tion nor Convenience to be connected with him in any shape, as, in all probability, he will be governed by the advice and Direction of that Adventurer.[1] His opinion of the work may be obtained at a smaller Risque. A particular friend of mine is well acquainted with Martinelli, but is now in Norfolk from whence he will return in a few weeks. I will then, if you please, commission him to talk with Martinelli on the subject of Dante, and whet his Curiosity in such a manner that he of himself shall beg a perusal of the Specimen. In that case it shall be read to him with those precautions you mention in your Letter to Ham.[2] If you desire that the affair should be otherwise conducted, be so good as to signify your Commands which shall be executed with Pleasure by,

> Kind sir,
> > your much obliged and affectionate humble Servt.,
> > > T! Smollett

I beg leave to present my best respects and warmest wishes to the Ladies, to Mr. Gatehouse[3] and Master Billy.[4] I have returned your letter to Martinelli.

Address: Not available. *Source:* MS. in HCSNJ. *First Printing:* By L. F. Powell in *Eighteenth Century Studies*, Spiral Press, New York, 1970.

Letter 55
To William Huggins

Chelsea, Augt. 2, 1758

Dear Sir,

I am much obliged to you for your present of Venison[5] which

Goldsmith, Dr. Johnson, and others when he was tried for murder in 1769 (Donald C. Gallup, 'Baretti's Reputation in England', in *The Age of Johnson Essays presented to Chauncey Brewster Tinker* (Yale University Press, 1949), 363–75). See also F. W. M. Draper, 'Johnson's Friend Baretti', in the *New Rambler*, no. B. XVI (Jan. 1965), 5–11. For the extraordinary relations, both friendly and inimical, between Baretti and Huggins, see Lacy Collison-Morley *Giuseppe Baretti* (London, 1909), 91–5.

[1] One who seeks chances of personal advancement. Smollett, in using this word, stressed its unfavourable connotations.

[2] Probably an abbreviation for Archibald Hamilton, Senior, the printer.

[3] Son-in-law of Huggins.   [4] The grandson of Huggins.

[5] 'What cannot Venison do?' declared Dr. James Grainger in accusing Smollett of partiality in his reviewing. See Grainger's *A Letter to Tobias Smollett* (London, 1759), 11, and footnotes, where he refers to Smollett's praise of Huggins' translation of Ariosto's *Orlando Furioso*. For details on Grainger's attack on Smollett, see Noyes, 180–2.

at

came safe to hand, though I am out of Countenance ~~for~~ [*sic*] the Trouble you gave yourself for my Pleasure and Convenience.

I condole you on the miserable weather by which our Spirits have been depressed these six weeks, but you are the less to be pitied as your situation is dry, and you can amuse yourself so agreeably within doors. When my friend comes to Town I will write you further concerning Martinelli.[1] I approve much of your specimen and scheme and intirely agree with you in the liking the stanza preferable to the common Metre. I beg my Compts. to the Ladies at Headly Park and to Mr. Monkhouse,[2] and I am (in some haste),

Dear Sir,

Your much obliged humble servt.,

T: Smollett

I thank you heartily for your kind concern touching my Health which at present is such that I have no Reason to complain.

Address: Not available. *Source:* MS. in HCSNJ. *First Printing:* By L. F. Powell in *Eighteenth Century Studies*, Spiral Press, New York, 1970.

Letter 56

To John Moore

Chelsea, Septr. 28 [? 1758]

Dear Sir,

I sometime ago was favoured with yours, which I should have answered sooner had not I been extremely busied in correcting my History for a new Impression.[3] That Task is now finished, and the Book, I hope, rendered less unworthy of the public Acceptance. I am much obliged to you for the generous warmth with which you have so often interposed in behalf of my Reputation. Of this, and every other Instance of Friendship which I have experienced at your hands, I shall ever retain a cordial Remembrance. I am not so much surprised at my Book's meeting with Censurers and Enemies

[1] See Letter 54, n. 5, p. 70.

[2] The Rev. Mr. Thomas Monkhouse, Fellow of the Queen's College, Oxford. See Powell, 179, n. 4.

[3] These corrections were made by Smollett in preparation for the publication of his *History* in 100 sixpenny numbers. Their sale was promoted by extensive publicity. See Knapp, 'The Publication of Smollett's *Complete History . . . and Continuation*', in *The Library*, the Bibliographical Society (London, 1935), 297–302. For the money Smollett received for his revisions (some £500) see R. M. Wiles, *Serial Publication in England Before 1750* (Cambridge University Press, 1957), 5–6.

in Glasgow as that it should find any number of Friends and Favourers among People so deeply infected with Prejudice and Fanaticism. I speak not of the few who think like Philosophers, abstracted from the notions of the Vulgar. The little petulant Familiarities of our friend Urie[1] I can forgive in consideration of the good will he has always manifested towards me and my Concerns. He is mistaken, however, in supposing I have imbibed priestly notions. I consider the Church not as a religious but as a political Establishment so minutely interwoven in our Constitution that the one cannot be detached from the other, without the most imminent danger of Destruction to both.[2]

The use which your friend makes of the Critical Review[3] is whimsical enough, but I shall be glad if he uses it at any rate. I have not had Leisure to do much in that work for some time past; therefore I hope you will not ascribe the articles indiscriminately to me for I am equally averse to the Praise and Censure that belong to other men. Indeed, I am sick of both and wish to God my circumstances would allow me to consign my Pen to oblivion. I really believe in my Conscience that mankind grows every day more and more malicious. I have taken some pains to live like an honest, inoffensive man; I will venture to say that nothing base or dishonourable can be justly charged upon my Character. Yet, I am daily persecuted by the most malicious slanders meerly because I have written with some Success. You will be not sorry to hear that the weekly Sale of the History has increased to above Ten thousand.[4] A french Gentleman of Talent and Erudition[5] has

[1] Robert Urie (Letter 20, n. 4, p. 32).

[2] Evidence for Smollett's belief that the Church was a political establishment is found in his account of the trial of Dr. Henry Sacheverel. (Noyes, 172, and *The Complete History of England*, iv 1758, 364–8.)

[3] This reference was explained by Dr. John Moore: 'I had written to Dr. Smollett that a friend of mine was so much enraged at some criticisms in that Review, that he continued to take it for no other purpose than that he might read all the publications censured by it, and none of those which it praised.' See Moore, I, clxiii, note.

[4] In the *Public Advertiser* (23 Dec. 1758), is a statement that the sale of the *History* was 'upwards of 10,000 weekly'.

[5] Probably Louis-Antoine Caraccioli (1721–1803), who was mentioned by David Hume in a letter to William Robertson as a person intending to translate Smollett's *History* (*The Works of W. Robertson, D.D.*, 1817, I, 169). Among the letters and documents kept by Smollett and sent after his death by the Rev. Thomas Hall of Leghorn to Dr. Benjamin Rusk of Philadelphia are several manuscripts of a French translation of short passages from Smollett's *History*. (These are now in the Historical Society of Pennsylvania, Du Simitière Papers, 967 F.) The name of the translator is not given. These translations are not identical with those of the same passages done by Jean-Baptiste Targe (1714–88), whose translation of Smollett's history in 19 volumes was published at Orleans, 1759–64.

undertaken to translate it into that Language, and I have promised to supply him with the Corrections. My best wishes are in behalf of Mrs. Moor and I am,

Dear John,
Yours affectionately,
T? Smollett

Address: To Mr. John Moor Surgeon in Glasgow North Britain. *Source:* MS. of PTS. *First Printing:* Partly printed by Moore, I, clxi–clxiii; Noyes, 54–5.

Letter 57

To Philip Miller

Chelsea, Jany. 20, 1759

Dear Sir,

If you are at Leisure I should beg as an addition to all your favours[1] your opinion of this late Performance of Hill's,[2] which I send with the Bearer, together with your Essay on the Papyrus;[3] your other Book I shall transmit one of these days. If we could have your Thoughts on the method of producing double Flowers from single, in a few days, so that they could be inserted in the number for this month,[4] it would be a double obligation on,

Sir,
your obliged, humble servt.,
T? Smollett

Address: To Mr. Philip Miller at his House in Chelsea. *Source:* MS. of Knapp. *First Printing:* By Knapp in *TLS* (24 June 1944), 312.

[1] The 'favours' received by Smollett from the eminent botanist, Philip Miller, F.R.S. (1691–1771) may well have included occasional book-reviews for the *Critical Review* (Knapp, 'Smollett's Letter to Philip Miller', *TLS* (24 June 1944), 312). Among Miller's books sold by S. Baker and G. Leigh, 12–15 Apr. 1774, was the *British Magazine*, 1760–7. See S.—C. S. 9 (4), B.M. Miller probably also contributed to this periodical.

[2] Dr. John Hill's *A Method of Producing Double Flowers from a Single* (London, 1758).

[3] Probably Miller's copy of Count de Caylus's *Dissertation sur le Papyrus* (Paris, 1758). A précis of this was printed in the *Critical Review*, vii (1759), 168–9.

[4] An unfavourable review, presumably by Miller, of Dr. Hill's book, appeared in the *Critical Review*, vii (1759), 118–23.

Letter 58
To John Wilkes[1]

Dear Sir,

I am again your Petitioner in behalf of that great Cham of Literature,[2] Samuel Johnson. His Black Servant, whose name is Francis Barber,[3] has been pressed[4] on board the Stag Frigate, Capt. Angel, and our Lexicographer is in great Distress. He says the Boy is a sickly Lad of a delicate frame, and particularly subject to a malady in his Throat which renders him very unfit for his majesty's Service. You know what matter of animosity the said Johnson has against you,[5] and I dare say you desire no other opportunity of resenting it than that of laying him under an obligation. He was humble enough to desire my asistance on this occasion, though he and I were never cater-cousins,[6] and I gave him to understand that I would make application to my Friend Mr. Wilkes who perhaps by his Interest with Dr. Hay and Mr. Elliot[7] might be able to procure the Discharge of his Lacquey. It would be superfluous to say more on the subject which I leave to your Consideration, but I cannot let slip this opportunity of declaring that I am with the most inviolable Esteem and Attachment,

Dear Sir,

your affectionate, obliged humble Servt.,

T: Smollett

[1] John Wilkes (1725–97), a very well-known wit and politician, M.P. and Lord Mayor of London, and the subject of many twentieth-century biographies. See George McCracken's article, 'John Wilkes, Humanist', *PQ*, xi (1932), 109–34. For his relations with Smollett prior to the break in their correspondence, see Noyes, 174–5.

[2] In *Roderick Random* (final paragraph of Ch. 56) Smollett alluded to the Cham (i.e. kahn or emperor) of Tartary. In the earliest publications of this letter, *Cham* was printed *Chum*. See *Letters between the Duke of Grafton . . . and John Wilkes, Esq. with Explanatory Notes*, vol. i, (1769), 59, and *Boswell's Life of Johnson*, revised by L. F. Powell, i (1934), 348–9.

[3] See *Boswell's Life of Johnson . . .*, revised by L. F. Powell, *passim*.

[4] Francis Barber was not forced into naval service.

[5] One possible reason for Johnson's dislike of Wilkes was the fact that Wilkes made fun of the lexicographer's amazing statement in his *Dictionary* that 'the letter H, seldom, perhaps never, begins any but the first syllable'. In 1755 Wilkes published anonymously an amusing comment which began as follows: 'The author of this observation must be a man of quick *appre-hension*, and of a most *compre-hensive* genius.' (Horace Bleackley, *Life of John Wilkes* (London, 1917), 38).

[6] Close friends.

[7] Dr. Hay (Sir George Hay, 1715–78), and Sir Gilbert Eliot were members of the Admiralty Board (Noyes, 177).

Address: Not available. *Source:* MS. in BM. *First Printing: Letters between the Duke of Grafton . . . and John Wilkes, Esq.,* no publisher, vol. i (1769), 59–60. It was also printed in *The St. James's Chronicle, or British Evening Post* (22–25 July 1769), and in *The Court Miscellany,* vol. v (July 1769), 352.

Letter 59
To John Wilkes

Chelsea, March 24, 1759

Dear Sir,

Ecce iterum Crispinus.[1] Your generosity with respect to Johnson[2] shall be the Theme of our applause and Thanksgiving. I shall be
your
very proud to find myself comprehended in ~~the~~ [*sic*] League offensive and defensive;[3] nay, I consider myself already as a contracting Party and have Recourse to the assistance of my Allies. It is not, I believe, unknown to you that Admiral Knowles[4] has taken Exception at a Paragraph in the Critical Review of last May[5] and commenced a Prosecution against the Printer.[6] Now, whatever termination the Trial may have, we shall infallibly be exposed to a considerable Expence, and therefore I wish to see the Prosecution quashed. Some Gentlemen who are my friends have undertaken to find out and talk with those who are supposed to have influence with the said Admiral. May I beg the same favour of you and your friends? The Trial will come on in the Beginning of May,[7] and if the affair cannot be compromised, we intend to kick up a dust and die hard. In a word, if that foolish Admiral has any regard for his own

[1] Behold Crispinus again (Juvenal, *Satire* IV, 1). This half-line, 'Ecce iterum Crispinus', became proverbial, meaning (a) that one returns to a topic already treated, or (b) that a theatrical character who left the stage for a moment returns to be seen (Larousse's *Grand Dictionnaire Universel Du XIXe Siècle,* 17 vols. (Paris, 1866–[90]), under *Crispinus*). Smollett is here using the first meaning, thus relating this letter to Letter 58.

[2] This refers to whatever Wilkes did to help secure Francis Barber's release from naval service.

[3] What is meant by Wilkes' *League* is not clear.

[4] Sir Charles Knowles (1704?–77). See *DNB*. Knowles was a violent and complex character, capable of contrasting interpretations, being involved in success and failure in his naval service, and also in duels and court-trials. For his portrait by John Faber, see Knapp, opposite p. 243.

[5] See *Critical Review,* v (May 1758), 438–9. See also Noyes, 177–8, and Knapp, *passim.*

[6] Archibald Hamilton, Senior, printer of the *Critical Review.*

[7] The trial was postponed until 24 Nov. 1760, when Smollett was fined £100 and sentenced to be imprisoned in the King's Bench (Prison) for three months.

character, he will be quiet rather than provoke further the Resentment of,

Dr. Sir,
your very obliged humble servt.,
T.⁵ Smollett

Address: Not available. *Source:* MS. in BM. *First Printing:* As for Letter 58.

Letter 60

To John Wilkes

Chelsea, April 1, [1759]

Dear Sir,

Nothing would give me more Pleasure than such an agreable opportunity of being known to Mr. Fitzherbert.[1] But I must at present deny myself that Pleasure in consequence of an Engagement a week old, which Engagement I should make no scruple of breaking on this occasion, if I were not on my good behaviour with some friend whom I dissappointed a Fortnight ago. As for Johnson I wish you may find[2] him sensible of the obligation he owes you. I desired my Printer to tell him what you had done with respect to his black servant; but I have heard nothing of his acknowledgement. On the Contrary I saw a very petulant Card which he had sent to the Printer concerning an Article in the last Review.[3] I am,

Dear Sir,
with inviolable Esteem and attachment,
your much obliged and obedt. servt.,
T.⁵ Smollett

I know you will not forget our affair with K———[4]

Address: Not available. *Source:* MS. in BM. *First Printing:* Whitridge, 125.

[1] William Fitzherbert of Tissington (1712–72), M.P. for Derby, friend of Wilkes, and a fellow-member of the Beef Steak Club.

[2] Noyes, 58, reads the very stained MS. as *make*, instead of *find*.

[3] If what Smollett calls the 'last Review' was that of Apr. 1759, then Johnson's 'petulant Card' may very possibly have referred to the review of his *The Prince of Abissinia*, later called *Rasselas*. This review was not wholly complimentary. See the *Critical Review* vii (Apr. 1759), 372–5.

[4] Admiral Charles Knowles (Letter 59, n. 4, p. 76).

(77)

Letter 61

To Samuel Richardson[1]

Chelsea, April 4, 1759

Dear Sir,

I have just received from your house eight printed sheets of the Modern History,[2] four of vol. xv. and four of vol. xvi, which I suppose have been written by Mr. Shirley;[3] but I protest I know not what I am to do with them. Pray, Sir, are these proof sheets to be corrected for the press, or are they already printed off? There is an intimation in the margin of the last page that Mr. Shirley goes no farther, and that you have been at a stand for several months. But this defect I cannot remedy until I shall have completed the chasm upon which I am at work; and now I talk of that chasm, I cannot help repeating my complaint that Dr. Campbell[4] should have left the task to me of filling up a chasm of fifteen or sixteen sheets, with a description of a country which all the art of man cannot spin out to half the number. I have before me all that ever was written on the subject, and find the task altogether impossible unless we throw into this place the discovery and description of the Straits of Magellan, Terra del Fuego, the Straits of Le Maire, Cape Horn, and an account of the voyages of some Navigators who have sailed round it into the South Sea. I do not see any impropriety in this expedient, as the subject naturally belongs to, or at least has an affinity with, that of the countries situated towards the Anntartic circle, and South Pole. I wish you would reflect upon this proposal, and favour me with your sentiments of it, that

---

[1] Samuel Richardson, printer and eminent novelist.

[2] The second or 'Modern Part' of the *Universal History*. It is likely that the detailed *Proposals for Publishing the Modern Part of the Universal History*, of which I have a copy (16 pp. octavo) issued 30 Nov. 1758, was prepared by Smollett as a part of his editorial duties. The forty-four volumes of the *Modern Part* were published from 1759 to 1766. Just how much writing in these volumes is by Smollett is uncertain, but he was supposed, according to Anderson (1820), 74, to have contributed to the histories of France, Italy, Germany, Denmark, Norway, Sweden, and Holland. His work as a compiler can not be determined.

[3] Probably William Shirley, a minor dramatist (fl. 1738–80). See *The Letters of David Garrick*, eds. David M. Little and George M. Kahrl—3 vols.; (The Belknap Press of Harvard University Press, 1963), ii, 483, n. 3.

[4] Dr. John Campbell (1708–75), a voluminous writer. For a long list of his works, historical, biographical, and political, see Robert Watt's *Bibliotheca Britannica* (1824), vol. i. Campbell was one of Johnson's Scottish friends.

To John Wilkes, 20 April 1759

I may proceed accordingly.¹ Meanwhile, I am, with inviolable esteem,

Dear Sir,
Your very humble servt.,
T⁹ Smollett

Address: To Mr. Richardson Printer—at his House in Fleet Street.
Source: Not located. *First Printing: Monthly Magazine,* vol. xlviii (1819), 326.

Letter 62
To John Wilkes

Chelsea, April 20, 1759

Dear Sir,

Were I not restrained by a sore Throat and consciousness of a Constitution
very capricious ~~Disposition~~, [*sic*] I should certainly avail myself of your kind Invitation. The Truth is I love the Country, especially at this Season, and I long to see your House at Aylesbury² as much as ever Akenside,³ or Gilbert Cooper,⁴ or any other wrong-headed Platonist longed to visit the Groves of Academus. I am sure I should there find much more agreable Company, and much better Chear than ever Plato, or at least than ever his master Socrates knew; nor, at your Table should I have any Reason to complain that the *Sal atticum*⁵ was wanting. But for the present I am obliged to enjoy these Pleasures in Speculation only; and even this feast of Imagination am I fain to snatch as a momentary Respite from reading dull books and writing dull Commentaries *invitâ Minerva,*⁶

¹ As Richardson was ill, he had his nephew, William Richardson, write a reply, dated 5 Apr. 1759, and published in the *Monthly Magazine,* vol. xlviii (1819), 326.
² The Prebendal House, near the manor-house and church at Aylesbury, Buckinghamshire.
³ The physician, Dr. Mark Akenside (1721–70). Smollett satirized him in *Peregrine Pickle,* but perhaps complimented him later. See Howard S. Buck, 'Smollett and Akenside', *JEGP,* xxxi (1932), 10–26.
⁴ John Gilbert Cooper (1723–69), miscellaneous writer, classical scholar, friend of Akenside, and a coxcomb, according to Edmond Malone, the editor of Shakespeare. Having heard that Cooper called him the Caliban of literature, Johnson said, 'I must dub him the Punchinello'. (Boswell's *Life of Johnson* . . . revised . . . by L. F. Powell, ii, 1934, 129.)
⁵ Attic salt, i.e. wit.
⁶ For *invitâ Minerva,* see Horace, *Epistles,* Book II, 3, 385. In this context, the phrase means 'against the grain of my natural abilities'. Many times Smollett expressed his boredom in working on the *Universal History.*

(79)

a Task almost as dissagreable as that of dining with our friend Armstrong, when the wind blows from the East, on a Loin of Veal roasted with Butter sauce.[1] I wish to God you who have so much Influence over our friend would persuade him to write an ode to *Eoster*, the Goddess of the East wind, so religiously cultivated by our Saxon Progenitors, especially in the month of April. It would doubtless be the finest Satire that ever appeared. It would contain the very Essence of peevish Delicacy [? inflamed] to a poetical Orgasm. I cannot express the Sense I have of all your Kindness or sufficiently acknowledge my obligation to you and Mr. Fitzherbert[2] for the Pains you have taken to pacify our incensed Admiral, who is, it seems, determined to proceed to Trial—but— *Turno tempis erit, magno cum optaverit emptum—intactum Pallanta.*[3] I wish you uninterrupted Happiness at Aylesbury, and indeed in such company I do not see how you can be otherwise than happy, and I am with unshaken attachment,

Dear Sir,

Your faithfull Servt.,

T! Smollett

Address: Not available. *Source:* MS. in BM. *First Printing:* Whitridge, 126.

Letter 63

To William Strahan

Chelsea, July 20, 1759

Dear Sir,

I should have answered the Letter you sent me some time ago, but conscious of my own Innocence with respect to some Insinuations therein contained, and of your entertaining some Jealousy

---

[1] Apparently Smollett did not share the fondness of his friend, Dr. John Armstrong, for veal, or for some other kinds of meat. In what was undoubtedly Smollett's review of Armstrong's *Sketches: or Essays on Various Subjects* (published under the pseudonym of Launcelot Temple, Esq; London, 1758) one reads: 'We likewise beg leave to differ from our author's opinion, that mutton has a more delicious flavour than venison; and that flounder is preferable to turbot. This, we conceive, is a downright solecism in eating, on which we should be glad to hold a practical conference with Mr. Launcelot Temple.' (Armstrong's *Sketches*, p. 9, and the *Critical Review*, v, 1758, 381.)

[2] See Letter 60, n. 1, p. 77.

[3] Quoted from Virgil's *Aeneid*, X, 503–4. It means 'the time will come when Turnus [i.e. Knowles] shall wish that Pallas, bought at so great a price, were unharmed'. This statement seems to imply that Smollett anticipated having future vengeance on Admiral Knowles (Noyes, 185).

which I knew Time and my Conduct would easily dissipate, I thought it would have been unnecessary to vindicate myself any other way from a Suspicion I had not justly incurred. I can say with a safe Conscience that, with respect to Mr. Strahan, I never once deviated from Those Thoughts which every honest man ought to entertain for an old friend to whom he has been essentially obliged.[1] You will never find any Just Reason to believe me capable of acting in another manner. I rejoice as much as ever in your Prosperity, and only regret that you are so little connected with me and so much with some Persons who I know to be my inveterate Enemies.[2] The first is not owing to any fault in me; nor do I impute the other to any abatement in your friendship for me, but to inevitable chances in the Course of Business. I wish you a great deal of Pleasure in your proposed Excursion; and shall take it kind, if when at Ed[inburgh], you will visit Commissary Smollett,[3] to whom and his Lady you will present my best respects. I repeat it that there is no Person on Earth who wishes you better than does,

Dear Sir,
Your obliged friend and servt.,
T: Smollett

Address: To Mr. William Strahan Printer in New Street. *Source:* MS. in PML. *First Printing:* Knapp, 'Smollett's Works as Printed by William Strahan with an Unpublished Letter of Smollett to Strahan', *The Library*, 4th Series, xiii (1932), 291.

[1] Smollett was of course grateful to the eminent printer, William Strahan, for his part in publishing his writings, including *Advice and Reproof*, 1748; *Roderick Random*, 1748; *Peregrine Pickle*, 1751; and the *History of England*. It is also probable that Smollett was assisted by his fellow-Scot in financial emergencies. For data on Strahan, see J. A. Cochrane, *Dr. Johnson's Printer The Life of William Strahan*, London, 1964.

[2] Smollett had in mind, presumably, Strahan's business contracts with persons like Ralph Griffiths, promoter of the *Monthly Review*, Dr. James Grainger, and other more obscure enemies. For Ralph Griffiths, see Knapp, 'Ralph Griffiths, Author and Publisher, 1746–1750', *The Library*, Bibliographical Society (London, 1939), 197–213. See also Benjamin Christie Nangle, *The Monthly Review First Series 1749–1789*, (Oxford, at the Clarendon Press, 1934), Preface.

[3] Smollett's cousin.

Letter 64
To John Wilkes

Chelsea Octr. 19, 1759

Dear Sir,

I am still an Invalid,[1] otherwise I would wait on you in person, and verbally sollicit your advice and asistance. K——[2] and his Friends talk of nothing but heavy Fines and Imprisonment. On the other hand, I am informed that in actions of this kind it is not uncommon for the Defendant to obtain of the attorney Genl.[3] a writt of noli prosequi,[4] as the Prosecution is carried on in the name of the Crown, and that the attorney Genl. on such occasions receives orders from the secretary of State. Nor is this any Hardship on the Plaintiff, as he has afterwards his Remedy at Common Law for any Damage he may have sustained by the pretended Libel. My dear sir, if you could think of any method of application to Mr. Pitt[5] that could give me any chance for obtaining such an Interposition, I flatter myself that you would, as usual, employ your Interest in behalf of,

Dear Sir,
Your much obliged and
affectionate humble servt.,
Tᵒ: Smollett

Address: Not available. *Source:* MS. in BM. *First Printing:* Whitridge, 127.

[1] The breakdown of Smollett's health seems to have been due primarily to the sedentary life made necessary by the incredible amount of work which he did in translating *Don Quixote*, in writing his *History of England*, and in composing an unknown number of reviews for the early years of the *Critical Review*, initiated in 1756.

[2] Admiral Charles Knowles.

[3] Charles Pratt (1714–94) an influential Whig, a friend of William Pitt, and later eminent as Lord Camden, was Attorney General in 1759.

[4] An entry made in a court record when the plaintiff abandons part, or all, of his suit against a defendant. See *nolle prosequi* in *OED*.

[5] William Pitt (1708–78), first Earl of Chatham, to whom Smollett dedicated his *History of England*. For Smollett's later relations with Pitt, see Knapp, 'Smollett and the Elder Pitt', *MLN* (Apr. 1944), 250–7.

Letter 65
To Dr. George Macaulay

Tuesday morning, Chelsea, Octr. 30, 1759

Dear Doctor,

I have had a Return of my Asthma in consequence of catching fresh cold. Otherwise I would this day wait on you in person. Mr. Jamieson[1] from Brussels was here, and I asked him if he had received the money for the Bill which I drew upon you from Flanders.[2] He answered that he knew nothing of the matter. I have forgot whether or not you payed it to his correspondent in London. In case you have not, he goes out of Town tomorrow, and I wish that affair was settled as he has behaved with great Friendship and Honour on the occasion. He lodges at Mr. Dobbins, Upholsterer in Conduit Street,[3] and I should take it as a particular Favour if you would call upon him. I long to know what steps you have taken with respect to Spain,[4] and am,

> Dear Sir,
> Your much obliged affectionate humble servt.,
> T? Smollett

Address: To Doctor Macaulay at his House [in] Jermyn Street. *Source:* MS. in NLS. *First Printing:* Anderson, 180–1.

Letter 66
To William Huggins

Chelsea, Novr. 27th, 1759

Dear Sir,

After a long Silence, the spirit moves me to pay my Respects to my kind and worthy friend of Headly Park where I have passed so many agreable Hours, and received so many Marks of his Friendship and Hospitality. I am sorry to find that an invidious rheumatic

---

[1] Unidentified.

[2] This refers to an unknown trip to Flanders taken by Smollett. The same journey (*c.* 1758–9) is possibly alluded to in his *Travels Through France and Italy*, Letter 1, paragraph 10.

[3] Unidentified.

[4] It is possible that Smollett was seeking a consulship in Madrid at this time. (Noyes, 187–8.) Why he could have been assisted by Dr. Macaulay is difficult to comprehend.

To William Huggins, 27 November 1759

Disorder has robbed you so long of my friend Monkhouse,[1] to whom I wrote a few Posts ago,[2] but I hope the Cold weather has had no such bad Effect upon the Ladies, to whom I present my most respectfull Compliments. Since I parted from you in the Country, I have read Berni[3] and the orlando furioso in the Italian from one end to the other, and was indeed become a sort of a Knight errant in Imagination.[4] Shall I tell you a secret? Notwithstanding the Extravagancies of Boyardo, I was so transported with some parts of him that my Hair stood on End. I wish I could see him Englished by such a Hand[5] as that which translated Ariosto. But no more of that. Hamilton[6] tells me you are resolved to turn Printer, and I wish you all the Success your Heart can desire. It will at least be a more rational Amusement than that of Electioneering, in which I see some of your neighbours are likely to be engaged. Before you left Wallop I had a letter from Mr Hill[7] giving me the Pleasure to know that his Fever had left him. I should have writt to Mr. Gatehouse[8] to acknowledge a present of Game,[9] but I wanted first to see Miss,[10] and durst not bring her to my House on acct. of my own child's[11] having the whooping Cough, of which she is hardly yet recovered. I shall, however, soon have the Pleasure to see her and then I can write with a better grace to the 'squire or his good Lady. Pray, make much of yourself in the cold weather, and allow me to be always,

Dear Sir,
your affectionate humble servt.,
T! Smollett

I shall send Berni[12] with the first safe Conveyance.

Address: Not available. *Source:* MS. in HCSNJ. *First Printing:* By L. F. Powell in *Eighteenth Century Studies*, Spiral Press, New York, 1970,

[1] See Letter 55, n. 3.
[2] This letter by Smollett has not been found.
[3] Francesco Berni (*c.* 1497–1535), a celebrated Italian poet who composed a new version of the *Orlando Innamorato* by Matteo Maria Boiardo (1541).
[4] Thanks to Smollett's knowledge of Latin, and possibly to some study of Italian because of his hours with Huggins, he would have been able to grasp much of the spirit of Berni's poetry.
[5] William Huggins.
[6] Archibald Hamilton, Senior, printer.
[7] Unidentified.
[8] Thomas Gatehouse, son-in-law of William Huggins.
[9] Probably venison.
[10] Presumably the daughter of Mr. and Mrs. Thomas Gatehouse.
[11] Elizabeth Smollett,
[12] The volume containing Berni's poem.

Letter 67
To John Harvie

Chelsea Dec. 10, 1759

Dear Sir,

'Procrastination (says a very gloomy author) is the thief of time',[1] and in this particular he says well. I know it by experience and plead guilty as an accomplice of the felon. As you observe, I owe you a long letter, and many other favours for which I shall always be in your debt. This, you will say, is the natural situation of an author. If I go on writing as I have proceeded for some years, my hand will be paralytic, and my brain dried to a snuff. I would not wish my greatest enemy a greater curse than the occupation of an author, in which capacity I have toiled myself into an habitual asthma, and been baited like a bear by all the hounds of Grubstreet. Some people have flourished by imputed wit; I have suffered by imputed dullness. I have been abused, reviled, and calumniated for satires I never saw; I have been censured for absurdities of which I could not possibly be guilty. But lest you should have reason to curse a correspondence which teems of nothing but disagreeable complaints, I will release you from the subject. We have received your last remittance per bill upon Sir Alexander Grant,[2] which was duly honoured, and likewise your subsequent intimation of a further remittance in silver, shipped on board of the Assistance.[3] I need not tell you how welcome these tidings have been; but it is my duty to tell you that all of us retain the most grateful sense of the kind attention you have given to our little affairs. Mrs. Leaver,[4] who seems to have renewed her age like the eagle,[5] is full of your praise; my wife is not silent on the subject, and you may be sure my heart will not fail to do you justice. Accept of their best compliments, joined to mine, presented to you and Mrs. ———,[6] to your brother Alick[7] and his partner, as also to

[1] Edward Young, *Night Thoughts*, Night I, line 393.
[2] Sir Alexander Grant (?–1772) became baronet in 1755 and was M.P. for Fortrose, Forress, Inverness, and Hairn (Scottish burghs) from 1761–68. He was also a London merchant.
[3] A ship listed in the *Journal of the Commissioners for Trade and Plantations, 1759–63*.
[4] Smollett's mother-in-law.
[5] This simile is found in *Peregrine Pickle*: 'Blessings on his old heart! one would think he had renewed his age, like the eagles.' See *The Adventures of Peregrine Pickle*, ed. James L. Clifford (London, Oxford University Press, 1964), 74.
[6] Probably Mrs. John Harvie.
[7] Alexander Harvie. (Knapp, 219, n. 99.)

To John Harvie, 10 December 1759

your brother William. I shall write to the doctor[1] by this opportunity. We have resolved, in compliance with your advice, to send
over a power for selling the negroes, and to transmit it by our old
friend Charles Sutty,[2] who is now bound for your island.

After having discussed my own business, give me leave to say
something in behalf of a friend. You doubtless remember Charles
————[3] with whom I have lived these eighteen years in the most
unreserved intimacy. He has been governor at Cape Coast, where
he acquitted himself nobly, and is going back to the same place in
the same character. I know him to be one of the best men that ever
were born, and I love him with the warmest affection. He tells me
his elder brother has fled from domestic unhappiness to your island,
and begs me to recommend him to your good offices. He knows not
well what scheme of life to pursue, and therefore will require your
advice and direction. Need I add that whatever civilities you shew
him, I shall consider as kindnesses done to my own brother. He
sailed from Scotland and will have been some time in Jamaica
before this comes to hand. I think he was bred to the Scotch law;
but as that is not practised in our colonies, I fancy he will be fit for
nothing but a clerk, or an overseer.

I flatter myself with the hopes of being happy in seeing your
brothers Alick and Tom[4] in England, but I am grieved to find you
determined upon a longer stay in the West Indies. I know not how
you may feel, but I perceive myself going down hill apace, and
promise myself but a few years of enjoyment. I would therefore

[1] Probably Dr. Thomas Harvie. In the manuscript letters to Samuel
Derrick in the Victoria and Albert Museum, London, there is a letter from one
Thos. Harvie (apparently a doctor) from Kingston, Jamaica, dated 27 June
1757. In this letter, Harvie thanked Derrick for his account of Smollett and
asked to be remembered to him. In a later letter from Sarum (near Salisbury,
England), dated 3 Mar. 1765, when Smollett was in Italy, Harvie wrote as
follows: 'I have not heard from Smollett for sometime myself, but C. Bell (see
n. 3) has had a late letter from him in which he seems to think his health is
reestablishing fast—I wish to God he would at last think of setting himself down
at Bath, where I hope we may enjoy many agreeable hours together. I know of
no body he could interfere with there but Doctor Gusthard and the Doctor is
too much of a gentleman to be affected by such selfish considerations. I dare say
he would receive Smollett with the open and extended arms of friendship.'

[2] Perhaps Charles Suttie, third son of Sir James Suttie of Balgone, in the
county of Fife. See William Robert Scott, *Adam Smith as Student and Professor*
(Glasgow, 1937), 37.

[3] Charles Bell, Governor of the Possessions on the Gold Coast, Africa, 1756–7,
and 1761–3. He was also on the Committee of the Company of Merchants
trading to Africa (*The Royal Kalendar; or, Correct Annual Register for England,
Scotland and Ireland for the Year 1767*, the 8th edn., corrected to 6 May 1767,
207). Smollett praised Bell's administrative courage and discretion in his
Continuation of the Complete History of England, ii (1760), 236–7.

[4] See n. 7, and n. 8.

make the most of my time and eagerly wish to see my friends about me. To tell you a secret, my constitution is quite broken. Since last May, I have hardly enjoyed one day of health. I am so subject to colds and rheums that I dare hardly stir from my own house, and shall be obliged to give up all the pleasures of society, at least those of tavern society, to which you know I have been always addicted.

The people here are in high spirits on account of our successes, and Mr. Pitt is so popular that I may venture to say that all party is extinguished in Great-Britain. That Minister is certainly in this respect the most surprising phenomenon that ever appeared in our hemisphere. If he had broke the spell by which we are bewitched to the continent, I would have pronounced him the greatest man that ever lived.

I have nothing more to say at present but that I am, my dear friend.

your most affectionate and obliged humble servant,
T. Smollett

Address: Not available. *Source:* MS. not located. *First Printing: The New Jamaica Magazine* (Feb. 1799), 115–16. See also Knapp, 'An Important Smollett Letter', in *RES*, xii (1936), 75–7.

Letter 68

To Mr. Richardson[1]

Chelsea, Feb. 4, 1760

Dear Sir,

Inclosed, I send a few remarks[2] on Mr. Richardson's paper; and if, after you and the other gentlemen concerned have perused them, you still shall think it expedient to publish a new account of the work,[3] according to our good friend's proposal,[4] I am ready to execute it to the best of my power. I likewise enclose a small list of books[5] for the History of Sweden. I have already got Puffendorf,[6]

[1] Either Samuel Richardson, or his nephew, William Richardson.

[2] The enclosed remarks by Smollett have disappeared.

[3] Probably the 'Modern Part' of the *Universal History*, repeatedly advertised at this time (Noyes, 190–1).

[4] Possibly a proposal by Andrew Millar, a proprietor of the *Universal History*.

[5] Books needed by Smollett.

[6] *The Compleat History of Sweden*, an English translation of a work by Samuel Puffendorf (1632–94), a German historian, was published in London in 1702.

(87)

the Memoirs of Queen Christina,[1] and an account of the Swedish Constitution, and am,

Sir, yours sincerely,
T.: Smollett

Address: Not available. *Source:* MS. not located. *First Printing: Monthly Magazine,* vol. xlviii (1819), 327.

Letter 69

To William Huggins

Chelsea, Feby. 24, 1760

Dear Sir,

You cannot doubt that your Asistance lent to any literary work in which I am engaged will always be agreable to me as well as to the Public. At present I am so enveloped in a variety of perplexing Schemes and Deliberations that I have neither Time to consider, nor Leisure to explain my sentiments of the manner in which the new Magazine[2] is to be executed and Improved. A great number of Essays both in prose and verse are sent to us from different parts of the Kingdom, but we have neither time to arrange them properly, nor give them that degree of alteration which we apprehend may be requisite to fit them for the public, and in all probability we shall be obliged to disappoint and give offence to some of our Correspondents. But these Inconveniences are inevitable in the prosecution of such a work with spirit and Candour. If you have by you any detached Pieces which you think will gratify the general Taste of Magazine Readers, we shall receive them with all due acknowledgement. I ought in this place to thank you once for all in consideration of repeated presents of Game[3] sent to me from Hampshire, and in particular to own the Receipt of an offering from Farmer Love[4] whose gratefull sense of the little service I did him[5] is

[1] *Memoirs Concernant Christine, Reine de Suède,* a French translation of a work by Johan Arckenholz (1695–1777), a Swedish historian, was published in four volumes, 1751–60.

[2] *The British Magazine or Monthly Repository for Gentlemen & Ladies,* the first number of which was scheduled to appear on New Year's Day 1760. Though Smollett was presumably the editor-in-chief, he was assisted by others, as is evident from the conclusion of the Dedication to William Pitt. See vol. i, p. ii, and Knapp, 221–3. No names of editors appeared on the title-pages of this periodical.

[3] Probably venison.

[4] Probably a farmer living on the property of William Huggins.

[5] Smollett seems to have given medical advice to Farmer Love.

very commendable, but such Gratification was quite superfluous and by me altogether unexpected. I must beg you will thank him in my name, and tell him that his Presents are quite unnecessary, for his Love[1] is sufficient. Please make a Tender of my Best respects to the Ladies. Let me be remembred to my worthy friend M_{ONK},[2] and set me down invariably yours,

T^s Smollett

Address: Not available. *Source:* MS. in HCSNJ. *First Printing:* By L. F. Powell in *Eighteenth Century Studies,* Spiral Press, New York, 1970.

Letter 70

To ? Samuel Richardson

Chelsea, May 1, 1760

Dear Sir,

You will receive with this the last part of the copy for France,[3] which was in my possession, and which brings the history no farther down than the year 1656, in the minority of Louis XIV. I suppose the rest of the copy must be with you or Mr. Millar.[4] You will see that in this parcel I have expunged many needless notes, abridged the text in divers places, and written side-notes where they were wanting; and all this with the great toil and hazard of my eyes; for, though the handwriting be very fine, it is also very small and extremely difficult to read. The great bulk of this copy arises, not from a great multiplicity of incidents and variety of matter, but from a certain spunginess of expression; and therefore cannot be properly pared unless we were to write the whole over again.[5] In writing the History of Sweden, we are at a great loss, and indeed a full stop, for want of the *Histoire General de Suede*,[6] which I wrote for to Mr. Millar several months ago. I am, with great sincerity and esteem, dear Sir, your very humble servant,

T^s Smollett

[1] An obvious pun.
[2] The Rev. Mr. Thomas Monkhouse (Letter 55, n. 3).
[3] The section on France in the 'Modern Part' of the *Universal History.*
[4] Andrew Millar, publisher.
[5] Smollett may have rewritten parts or all of the section on France attributed to him by his biographer Dr. Robert Anderson, who, however, furnished no documentary evidence.
[6] The author of this volume is still to be identified.

I should think myself happy if you would favour our Magazine[1] with any loose essay lying by you which you do not intend for another sort of publication.

[T.[s] Smollett]

Address: Not available. *Source:* MS. not located. *First Printing: Monthly Magazine,* vol. xlviii (1819), 327.

Letter 71

To ? Samuel Richardson

Chelsea, May 31, 1760

Dear Sir,

As the authors who treat of Sweden[2] cannot be procured, I must either lay the work aside, or proceed to another subject. I have pitched upon Holland,[3] and inclosed a list of books which I beg may be sent with all expedition, as both I and my amanuensis[4] are idle in the meantime.

I am with great esteem,
Sir, your very humble servant,
Ts. Smollett

Address: Not available. *Source:* MS. not located. *First Printing: Monthly Magazine,* vol. xlviii (1819), p. 327, which is followed here.

Letter 72

To William Huggins

Chelsea, July 12, 1760

Dear Sir,

I seize this short opportunity of paying my Respects to you before I set out for the North[5] where I shall stay a few weeks; but

---

[1] *The British Magazine* (Letter 69, n. 2, p. 88).

[2] See Letter 68.

[3] It is possible that Smollett wrote the section on Holland in the 'Modern Part' of the *Universal History.*

[4] Unidentified.

[5] Smollett arrived in Edinburgh in time to receive in person the honour of being appointed 'Burges and Gildbrother' on 30 July 1760 (Knapp, 229). This honour had been first awarded him in Edinburgh in 1753 (Kahrl, 62). When Smollett returned to London is not known. His next and last trip to Scotland was in 1766.

for all that Journey I shall not resign the Hope of seeing my Friends at Headly Park before the end of Autumn. You may believe me when I assure you no Place affords me more heartfelt satisfaction. I am sorry to hear of my friend Jack's[1] Indisposition which I'm afraid will terminate in a Consumption. I beg you will conceal this opinion from his Knowledge. I have herewith enclosed a Prescription, but I should depend more upon Riding than on any pharmaceutical composition. I wish he may not have lost too much Blood. Let his Diet be light and moderate in quantity, and if the Sweats should be found not critical but weakening, he ought to rise very early in the morning to prevent their bad Effect. Please communicate my Compts. to the Ladies and my friend Monkhouse,[2] and do me the justice to believe that I am with the warmest esteem and affection,

Dear Sir,
Your very humble servt.,
T^s Smollett

Should the pills agree with Jack he may increase the Dose to six, morning and evening.

Address: Not available. *Source:* MS. in HCSNJ. *First Printing:* By L. F. Powell in *Eighteenth Century Studies,* Spiral Press, New York, 1970.

Letter 73

To ? Samuel Richardson

Chelsea, Octr. 12, 1760

Dear Sir,

I have dropped a few Hints on the other Leaf[3] which you will please to cast your Eye upon before you meet the other Proprietors of the Universal History. I think it my Duty to submit them to your Opinion, as well as to caution you against any Proprietor who may have an Interest in pressing a Discontinuance of the work from

---

[1] Unidentified.

[2] See Letter 55, n. 2, p. 72.

[3] Though this leaf of the letter has disappeared, the 'Hints for the Consideration of the Proprietors of the Universal History' were printed in the *Monthly Magazine,* vol. xlviii (1819), 328, under the heading, 'Thoughts on the Universal History'. In these hints Smollett offers explanations for the decreasing sale of the 'Modern Part' of the *Universal History,* and submits suggestions for helping the proprietors regain their financial losses (Noyes, 193).

(91)

a View to be concerned in a Rival Performance[1] set up against the Universal History. For my own part I declare myself altogether uninterested in your Determination, as I can always employ my Time to much greater advantage than I could possibly reap from the Completion of this work, and am now fully resolved to have no new Engagements with the Proprietors in any Scheme of Abridgement. At least I shall never tie up my hands in such a manner as to render myself a slave for Life to a work which I should never live to accomplish. Other Tradesmen can acquire wealth by employing a number of good Hands under their immediate Direction, but an Author of Genius and Reputation must, it seems, be a Journeyman[2] for Life, and be obliged to subsist by the Labour of his own Hands. Such Doctrine I know your generous Heart disdains. You pay a more proper Respect to Learning and Ingenuity, to that class of writers among whom you yourself possess such superior Rank

of

and unenvied Eminence. But such are the maxims ~~by which~~ [*sic*] a set of contemptible Reptiles who have enriched themselves by works which have scarce afforded their Authors the necessaries of Life. I am with the utmost Deference and Esteem,

> Dear Sir,
> Your very humble Servt.,
> Tᵒ Smollett

Address: Not available. *Source:* MS. in BM. This MS. has lines drawn through the last five sentences. In the left-hand margin of the first four sentences of the letter there are quotation marks; there are also brackets within the letter. It is not known who added these lines, quotation marks, and brackets. *First Printing: Monthly Magazine,* vol. xlviii (1819), 327–28.

Letter 74
Letter of Appeal to Lord Mansfield[3]

c. November 24, 1760

My Lord,

I beg to be indulged with a few Words in Justification of some parts of my Conduct which I apprehend have been misrepresented

---

[1] Nothing is available concerning this rival performance, or publication, which never appeared.

[2] A day-labourer, hireling, or drudge. In *Peregrine Pickle*, Smollett describes literary 'day-labourers', the victims of tyrannical booksellers, in the opening paragraphs of chapters ci and cii of the first edition. See *Peregrine Pickle*, ed. James L. Clifford (London, Oxford University Press), 637 and 645.

[3] William Murray (1705–93), first Earl of Mansfield, and Chief Justice of the King's Bench (1756–88).

and misunderstood. This Indulgence I the more earnestly intreat, as my Silence when last I was before your Lordship[1] may have been interpreted into Contumacy or Want of Respect for the Authority of this Court which I ever did and always shall revere with the most profound Veneration and Submission. What might be imputed to me in this respect as a Crime was really my Misfortune. My being produced in the Character of a Delinquent before such an awful Tribunal had such an Effect upon my Spirits that I was really deprived of the Power of Utterance.

It has been urged, My Lord, as a Proof of my Malignity and Contempt of the Law that when the Printer[2] was prosecuted for the Paragraph which has been adjudged a Libel,[3] and the Cause was brought to a Hearing before your Lordship, I took the Advantage of an Expression dropped by one of Mr. Knowles's[4] Council and owned myself in open Court Author of that offensive Paragraph in Defiance of the Law and in order to involve Mr. Knowles in the Expence and Trouble of a fresh Prosecution. Thus, My Lord, have I been stigmatized for a Step which I humbly Conceive Your Lordship, when my Motives are explained, will ascribe to a good and honourable Intention; I understood that Mr. Knowles had a double Action, an Action against the Author as well as the Printer of the Paragraph in Question. My Humanity and Friendship were interested for the Printer whom I had unwillingly involved in Trouble, and I thought I could not in Conscience do too much for his Indemnification. Mr. Knowles by the Mouth of his Council declared that if the Printer would give up the Author he would then withdraw the Prosecution from him. I had desired our Council to embrace this Proposal if it should be made. The Proposal was made and embraced accordingly, and then I was suddenly ordered to appear in Court so contrary to my Expectation, so much against my Will that I was never so surprised and mortified in the whole Course of my Life; far from being in a Condition to shew any Contempt for the Law or the Prosecutor on that Occasion, I was for some Minutes so discomposed that all my Faculties were suspended. The Endeavours that I used in the Sequel to effect an Accomodation, and the Offer I made to pay the Prosecutor's Costs will convince Your Lordship that the Charge of Obstinacy is unjust, and that I had no Design to accumulate the Expence of

---

[1] The precise time is uncertain; it may have been on 25 June 1760, when the sheriff of Middlesex carried out his order to bring Smollett to Westminster Hall. See Alice Parker, 'Tobias Smollett and the Law', *SP*, xxxix (1942), 552.

[2] Archibald Hamilton, senior.

[3] See the *Critical Review*, v (1758), 438.

[4] Admiral Charles Knowles. See Letter 59, n. 4, p. 76.

Mr. Knowles. That my subsequent Conduct with respect to this unhappy Affair has been unjustly branded with the Epithets— Malicious and Obstinate—appears from the Concessions I not only offered but actually made to the Prosecutor, Concessions suggested by his own Solicitor, approved and recommended by his own Council as well as by his particular Friend, the late Lord Register of Scotland.[1] I agreed to pay a Considerable Sum of mony [*sic*] in Lieu of his Costs. I wrote a Letter asking his pardon in the Terms dictated by his own Friend, the Lord Register. The Letter was written, signed, sealed and directed in presence of his own Solicitor[2] and deposited in the hands of Dr. Baylies[3] to be forwarded to Mr. Knowles whenever he should signify his Approbation and Desire of terminating the affair.

I shall trouble Your Lordship with nothing further on this Occasion than to declare my hearty Sorrow for having offended the Laws of my Country, my Readiness to make all the Atonement in my Power to the injured Party by any Concessions that shall be thought just, and my perfect Submission[4] to your Lordship's Authority.

T: Smollett

Address: Not available. *Source:* MS. in Public Record Office, King's Bench, 1/14, Michaelmas Term, 1, George III. This is probably a clerk's copy, clearly signed by Smollett. *First Printing:* Knapp's 'Rex versus Smollett: More Data on the Smollett–Knowles Libel Case', *MP*, xli (May 1944), 221–7.

Letter 75
To William Huggins

c. 1760

Dear Sir,

I congratulate you heartily on the stupendious work you have finished,[5] and hope the success of it with the Public will make ample amends in Fame and Reputation for the herculean Labours

---

[1] The Hon. Alexander Hume Campbell, Lord Register of Scotland (Letter 14, n. 1, p. 21).

[2] Probably John Chapone.

[3] William Baylies, M.D. (1724–87) (Knapp, 232, n. 44).

[4] Smollett's submission had some effect on Lord Mansfield (Knapp, 232, n. 46).

[5] This may refer to Huggins' lost translation of Dante. For a very short extract from it see the *British Magazine*, i (Apr. 1760), 266.

you have undergone. After all, I rather admire than approve of that Perseverance in Trouble, by which a man unnecessarily impairs his

which has

Health and Faculties for the Entertainment of a Public ~~without~~ [*sic*] neither Taste or Discernment, without any other View of Recompence than the precarious Hope of a little transient applause which I take to be one of the most unsubstantial Enjoyments of Life, if that may be called an Enjoyment which we cannot have pure and undisturbed by the censure of jealous Envy and petulant Ignorance. I think your mottos[1] are very well chosen; and I much approve of your Design to print a small number only for the use of your Friends. In this case the Translation will be handed about as a Curiosity which may inflame the Impatience of the Public, and thus pave the way for the sale of a large Impression.

You tell me that your Finnances are otherwise engaged, and ask my opinion with respect to the Prosecution of your printing scheme. It is then my opinion that you should postpone that and every other scheme of amusement (for such I apprehend it to be) that will be attended with the least anxiety of Thought, or the smallest Difficulty of Execution. The very Design (which is that of pleasing yourself) will be perverted by a contrary Conduct, and that which ought to constitute your Happiness will be productive of Mortification and Disquiet. Alas! why should a man who can live in Ease and Tranquility, exercising the Virtues of Benevolence, and full-filling all the Duties of social Life, torment himself with troubles over Schemes of literary ambition, embark in a whiffling[2] Lottery of Public Praise, containing a thousand mortifying Blanks for one Prize of little Value, and expose himself to the Torrent of opposition swelled by the different streams of Satire, Ridicule and Misrepresentation? For my part, I long eagerly for some quiet, obscure Retreat, where, as from a safe and happy Harbour, I may look back with self gratulation, upon that stormy Sea of Criticism[3] in which my little Bark has been so long and so violently tossed and afflicted. I cannot without Mortification reflect that it is in the power of the lowest Reptile to asperse my Morals as a man, and impeach my Reputation as a writer. If I neglect the charge, my silence is interpreted into conscious Guilt or Imbecillity. If I justify my conduct and character, I am taxed with acting meanly in con-

[1] Heading the extract referred to in n. 5, p. 94. is a Latin motto, 'Sicut meus mos', taken apparently from Horace, *Sermones*, Liber I, ix, l. 1: 'Ibam forte Via Sacra, sicut meus est mos.'

[2] Windblown.

[3] Smollett had received by 1760 a great many indirect and personal attacks because of his editorship of the *Critical Review*. For a list of these attacks, see Claude E. Jones, *Smollett Studies*, (University of California Press, 1942), 107–11.

descending to wrestle with such a vile Antagonist. Believe me, Sir, I could say a thousand things on the same Subject dictated from a Feeling sore with repeated Injuries, but I have not Leisure to say any thing more at present, except that I am with great cordiality, your affectionate humble servt.,

T:S Smollett

Be so good as to receive for yourself, and transmit to the Ladies, as well as to friend Monkhouse,[1] the compliments of the season which I present from a Heart warm with Esteem and acknowledgement.

Address: Not available. *Source:* MS. in HCSNJ. *First Printing:* By L. F. Powell in *Eighteenth Century Studies*, Spiral Press, New York, 1970.

Letter 76

To William Huggins

Chelsea Feby. 25, 1761

My dear and much respected Friend,

I have not been so deeply affected these many years as I was when I received your last kind Favour.[2] Believe me, Sir, my Heart swells, and even my Eyes overflow, with Tenderness, when I now review the Contents. I flattered myself with the Hope of being able to present myself at your gate, unexpected, and surprise you with my personal Congratulation on your Recovery. I hope to do it still. At present, Headly Park has no charms for me. I should miss my kind Landlord and be miserable. You say nothing of your Health, yet I have been informed it is on the mending hand. Pray, desire Mr. Gatehouse[3] or any Friend to give me some Description of your Case, and tell me whether the water agrees with you. If not, to what purpose stay at Bath? I am perplexed and uneasy, and have no Joy in Liberty, while my good Friend is disordered or dejected. Were I not tied down to the stake by periodical Publications, I would pay my respects to you in Somersetshire. Who is your Physician? What Regimen do you observe? Forgive my want of

[1] See Letter 55, n. 2, p. 72.

[2] Precisely what this 'Favour' was is unknown, but it may have been Huggins' offer, in his letter to Smollett of 21 Feb. 1761, of a free apartment (Powell, 188).

[3] Sir Thomas Gatehouse, son-in-law of Huggins. Gatehouse was knighted in 1762, according to the *Gentleman's Magazine*, lxxxvi (1816), I, 321. See also Powell, 189.

Connexion. Receive my Sincere Thanks for your generous Invitation, and believe me to be with invariable Esteem and warmest affection,

My dear Sir,
Your very humble Servt.,
T<u>s</u> Smollett

I offer my best Respects to Mrs. Gatehouse, not forgetting our kind Landlord of Wallop,[1] whose Generosity made the Bells of Chelsea ring at my Deliverance.[2]

Address: To Wm. Huggins Esqr. at his House in Chapel Row Queen Square Bath Somersetshire. *Source:* MS. in HCSNJ. *First Printing:* Powell, 189.

Letter 77

To David Garrick

Chelsea, April 5, 1761

Dear Sir,

I see Mr. Colman[3] has taken offense at the article in the Critical Review which treats of the Rosciad,[4] and I understand he suspected me to be author of that article. Had he asked me the question I should have freely told him I was not the author of the offensive article, and readily contributed to any decent scheme which might have been proposed for his satisfaction. But as he has appealed to

---

[1] Sir Thomas Gatehouse.

[2] This ringing of the church-bells of Chelsea when Smollett came home from prison in late Feb. 1761, was probably part of a 'general illumination' (the lighting up of the houses in Chelsea). According to local tradition, Smollett was honored by another 'general illumination' in 1753 when he was freed from charges of assault in the lawsuit with Gordon and Groom.

[3] George Colman, the elder (1732–94), was a writer of verse, a successful dramatist, and a friend of Garrick and of Charles Churchill. From 1767–77 he was manager of the Covent Garden Theatre and later was manager of the Haymarket Theatre. From 1764 to 1789 he wrote reviews for the *Monthly Review*. In 1761 he initiated the *St. James's Chronicle*, and in 1770 he wrote Smollett a friendly letter asking about a play which Smollett had previously planned to submit to him. See List of Letters to Smollett.

[4] See the *Critical Review*, xi (Mar. 1761), 209–12; and also xi (Apr. 1761), 339. Colman was irritated by this review in which it was suggested that he, in conjunction with Robert Lloyd and Bonnell Thornton, wrote the *Rosciad*, utilizing this clever but abusive satire of inferior actors as a means of publicizing and praising himself. See Noyes, 195.

(97)

the public,[1] I shall leave him and the real author[2] to settle the affair between themselves, and content myself with declaring to you, and that upon my honour, that I did not write one word of the article upon the Rosciad; that I have no ill-will nor envy to Mr. Colman, whom I have always respected as a man of genius, and whose genius I shall always be ready and pleased to acknowledge either in private or public. I envy no man of merit, and I can safely say I do not even repine at the success of those who have no merit. I am old enough to have seen and observed that we are all playthings of fortune, and that it depends upon something as insignificant and precarious as the tossing up of a halfpenny whether a man rises to affluence and honours, or continues to his dying day struggling with the difficulties and disgraces of life. I desire to live quietly with all mankind, and if possible to be upon good terms with all those who have distinguished themselves by their extraordinary merit. I must own that if I had examined the article upon the Rosciad before it was sent to the press, I should have put my negative on some expressions in it, though I cannot see in it any reflection to the prejudice of Mr. Colman's moral character; but I have been so hurried since my enlargement[3] that I had not time to write one article in the Critical Review except that upon Bower's History,[4] and perhaps I shall not write another these six months. That hurry and a bad state of health have prevented me from returning in person the visit you favoured me with in the King's Bench.[5] I beg you will accept this letter in lieu of it, and believe that no man respects Mr. Garrick more than he is respected by his obliged humble servant,

T. Smollett

Address: Not available. *Source:* MS. not located. *First Printing: Plays and Poems written by T. Smollett, M.D.* (London, 1777), xvii–xix.

[1] Soon after the appearance in Mar. 1761 of the article in the *Critical Review* (see n. 4, p. 97), Colman disclaimed in the newspapers any share of the authorship of the *Rosciad.*

[2] Charles Churchill (1731–64), the well-known satirical poet, clergyman, and friend of John Wilkes.

[3] Release from the King's Bench prison.

[4] For Smollett's brilliant attack on Archibald Bower's *The History of the Popes . . . vol. V,* see the *Critical Review,* xi (Mar. 1761), 217–33. It is almost certain that Smollett wrote or approved some of the reviews in the *Critical Review* (see vols. i–v) which denounced Bowers as an extraordinary imposter.

[5] For other persons who may have visited Smollett in prison, see Knapp, 236.

Letter 78
To William Huggins

Chelsea, May 8, 1761

Dear Sir,

I presume I need not expatiate on the Pleasure I felt at receiving your last Favour, in which I have it under your own hand that you are now on the Recovery. For God's sake comport yourself with that Delicacy of Regard, that punctual attention to the Directions of your Physician, which may exempt you from all Hazard of Relapse. My Satisfaction is still mingled with a tender apprehension which will not be totally removed untill your Health shall be perfectly reestablished. When I receive that agreable Intimation, I will endeavour to steal from my Engagements a short Visit to my worthy Friends. Meanwhile I commit you to the Direction of your Doctor, the Care and Tenderness of Mrs. Gatehouse, the Prayers and Wishes of all who have the Happiness of your Acquaintance and Friendship, among whom I take pleasure in numbering

Dear Sir,
Your very affectionate humble Servt.,
T? Smollett

My best Respects are offered to Mrs. and Mr. Gatehouse,[1] and all good friends at Wallop.[2]

Address: Not available. *Source:* MS. in HCSNJ. *First Printing:* Powell, 190.

Letter 79
To William Huggins

Chelsea, May 25, 1761

My dear Sir,

Hamilton[3] tells me he left you in good spirits, though very weak and much emaciated, and even inclined to change your Physician, a step which I know you will not take precipitately. If you have a favourable opinion of another, let the two Doctors consult together, and Heaven grant a Blessing to their Prescription. I long extremely

---

[1] Sir Thomas Gatehouse, son-in-law of Huggins.
[2] Huggins had recently returned from Bath to Wallop.
[3] Probably Archibald Hamilton, the well-known publisher.

to see you and would fain make an excursion sometime next week to Wallop if I could break away from my slavish Engagements. Meanwhile, I beg to hear in what manner you proceed with respect to the Recovery of your Health, which, I hope, I need not say, is an affecting Consideration to

Dear Sir,

Your very affectionate humble servt.,

T: Smollett

My best respects to Mr. and Mrs. Gatehouse[1] and all friends at Wallop.

Address: Not available. *Source:* MS. in HCSNJ. *First Printing:* Powell, 190.

Letter 80

To Thomas Gatehouse[2]

Chelsea, June 9, 1761

My dear Squire,

Hamilton[3] at his return from Wallop gave me such a discouraging account of my worthy Friend that I changed my Resolution of going into Hampshire because I could not have bore the shock of seeing him in such a hopeless Situation. I can safely say that I never was more affected by the Loss of the nearest Relation that I should be upon losing Mr. Huggins whom I have ever loved with the most cordial affection. I sincerely pity Mrs. Gatehouse[4] whose tender Heart must be deeply impressed by the prospect of losing such an indulgent and amiable Parent. It will therefore be incumbent on you, my dear Squire, to redouble your attention and Tenderness in your Endeavours to alleviate her Loss. But I know there is no occasion to remind you of that Duty. I beg leave to present my best respects to her, and to be remembred to all my friends at Wallop, not forgetting Monk[5] if he is still with you. Excuse Haste and believe me to be with inviolable Sincerity, Dear Sir,

Your affectionate humble Servt.,

T: Smollett

[1] See Letter 80, n. 4.
[2] Sir Thomas Gatehouse, son-in-law of Huggins.
[3] See Letter 79, n. 1.
[4] Huggins' daughter, Anna Maria, who married Gatehouse in 1747.
[5] The Rev. Thomas Monkhouse (Letter 55, n. 2, p. 72).

(100)

Address: Not available. *Source:* MS. in HCSNJ. *First Printing:* Powell, 191.

Letter 81
To Thomas Gatehouse[1]

Chelsea, June 14, 1761

Dear Sir,

I take this first opportunity of inquiring once more concerning the Condition of my good friend Mr. Huggins,[2] and of offering him the best wishes that my Heart can form. I must also make some apology for having left you so abruptly that I did not even pay my Respects to Mrs. Gatehouse who is so worthy of all Respect, Honour and affection. The truth is I was in such Confusion that I hardly knew what I did; and in consideration of the Cause of that Confusion I know she will excuse my involuntary neglect. At Farnham[3] I was so ill of the Asthma that I really began to think seriously of Suffocation, but I am now considerably mended. I saw our friend Monkhouse,[4] and reconnoitred Viner's House at aldershot,[5] which will not do for my Purpose.[6] Finally I arrived without accident at Chelsea where I found my Family in good Health, tho' our old Gentlewoman[7] had such a scouring[8] in my absence that my wife thought she could not have lived till my Return. But she is now perfectly recovered and I am content. Whatever might have happened, you know I must have acquiesced in the Dispensations of Providence.[9] I present my Compts. and best wishes to Mrs. Gatehouse, Miss Huggins,[10] my dear miss Gatehouse,[11] and good Mrs. Erskine,[12] to Dr. Musgrave[13] whose acquaintance I should be

---

[1] Son-in-law of William Huggins.

[2] William Huggins died 3 July 1761, aged sixty-five (Powell, 192, n. 42).

[3] Farnham, Surrey, where Smollett stopped on his return from Nether Wallop to Chelsea.

[4] See Letter 55, n. 2, p. 72.

[5] Probably the property of Charles Viner, a benefactor of Oxford, who had died in 1756 (Knapp, 239, n. 77).

[6] Smollett's purpose in regard to inspecting Viner's house is unknown.

[7] Probably Smollett's mother-in-law, Mrs. Elizabeth Leaver, who died in Chelsea in 1762 (Knapp, 265, n. 3).

[8] Diarrhoea.

[9] Smollett, it seems, was not much attached to his mother-in-law (Letter 13).

[10] Maria Anna, Huggins' youngest daughter (Powell, 189, n. 30, and 191, n. 36).

[11] Anna Maria, second child of Thomas Gatehouse. See Powell, 192, n. 37.

[12] The Hon. Mrs. Annabella Erskine, to whom Huggins willed an annuity of £30 (Powell, 192, n. 38).

[13] Dr. James Musgrave, son-in-law of William Huggins. For more data about this person, see Powell, 192, n. 39.

proud to cultivate, to my worthy friend Hill,[1] and to Mr. Cotton[2] whose distemper is, I hope, by this time abated. Let me be also remembred to Masters Sawney and Billy,[3] and believe me to be with all Sincerity of affection,

My dear Squire
Your most obedt. Servt.,
T.[S] Smollett

Address: Not available. *Source:* MS. in HCSNJ. *First Printing:* Powell, 191–2.

Letter 82
To John Wilkes

Chelsea, Novr. 2, 1761

Dear Sir,

If I was not remarkably interested in behalf of the Bearer, I would not give you this Trouble. His name is Robert Love,[4] son of the man from whose Instruction I imbibed the first Principles of my Education.[5] He has been bred to the Sea, and acted as a petty officer on board of a King's Ship to the entire Satisfaction of his Commander, as will appear from the Certificates which he can produce. He has distinguished himself in some desperate Pieces of Service, particularly in boarding the french Ships in Louisbourg Harbour,[6] and in attacking with Boats two Privateers in Cumberland Harbour[7] on the Island of Cuba. He was sent home from Jamaica, Commander of a considerable Prize, and has lately passed Examination as a Lieutenant, but being utterly destitute of Interest,[8] I presume to recommend him to your good offices, and will vouch for his being a brave, honest and skillfull mariner. Shall I beg the favour of your mentioning him to Dr. Hay,[9] or any other member of the Board of Admiralty? I should think there would be no great difficulty in procuring a Commission for such a man at a time when Seamen are so much in Request. I know you will forgive

---

[1] The Rev. Edward Hill, to whom Huggins bequeathed gifts.

[2] A witness of Huggins' will.

[3] Alexander and William Gatehouse, sons of Sir Thomas Gatehouse (Powell, 192, n. 41).

[4] George Chalmers, in his *Life of Thomas Ruddiman* (London, 1794), p. 135, referred to Robert Love as being in the navy. Neither the date nor Love's rank was given.

[5] See Letter 5, n. 2, p. 7.   [6] See Noyes, 197.   [7] See Noyes, 197.

[8] Influence with the Board of Admiralty.   [9] See Letter 58, n. 7, p. 75.

this Freedom, and allow me to be, with the most perfect Esteem and affection,

> Dear Sir,
> Your much obliged and most obedt. servt.,
> T: Smollett

Address: Not available. *Source:* MS. in BM. *First Printing:* Whitridge, 128.

Letter 83

To David Garrick

Chelsea, Jan. 27, 1762

Dear Sir,

I this morning received your Winter's Tale,[1] and am agreeably flattered by this mark of your attention. What I have said of Mr. Garrick in the History of England[2] was, I protest, the language of my heart. I shall rejoice if he thinks I have done him barely justice. I am sure the Public will think I have done no more than justice. In giving a short sketch of the liberal arts, I could not, with any propriety, forbear mentioning a gentleman so eminently distinguished by a genius that has no rival. Besides, I thought it was a duty incumbent on me in particular to make a public attonement in a work of truth for wrongs done him in a work of fiction.[3]

Among the other inconveniencies arising from ill-health, I deeply regret my being disabled from a personal cultivation of your good will, and the unspeakable enjoyment I should sometimes derive from your private conversation as well as from the public exertion of your talents; but sequestered as I am from the world of

---

[1] *Florizel and Perdita; Or The Winter's Tale. A Dramatic Pastoral . . . Altered from Shakespear. By David Garrick . . .* (London, 1762). The copy sent to Smollett had been published within a few weeks, and was very favourably reviewed, probably by Smollett, in the *Critical Review*, xiii (Feb. 1762), 157–8.

[2] Garrick sent Smollett a copy of his alteration of the *Winter's Tale* probably in response to Smollett's tribute to him in the *Continuation of the Complete History of England*, iv (1761), 126. A part of the tribute ran as follows: '[Garrick] greatly surpassed all his predecessors of this, and perhaps every other nation, in his genius for acting; in the sweetness and variety of his tones; the irresistible magic of his eye; the fire and vivacity of his action; the elegance of attitude; and the whole pathos of expression.'

[3] *Peregrine Pickle* (1751). In the second edition (1758), Smollett had excised his satire of Garrick's acting.

entertainment, the consciousness of standing well in your opinion will ever afford singular satisfaction to,

Dear Sir,
Your very humble Servant,
T. Smollett

Address: Not available. *Source:* MS. not located. *First Printing: Plays and Poems written by T. Smollett, M.D.* (London, 1777), pp. iv–v.

Letter 84

To John Wilkes

Chelsea, March 28, 1762

Dear Sir,

My warmest Regard, affection and attachment you have long ago secured. My Secrecy you may depend upon. When I presume to differ from you in any point of opinion, I shall always do it with Diffidence and Deference.[1] I have been ill these three months, but hope soon to be in a condition to pay my Respects to Mr. Wilkes in Person. Mean while I must beg leave to trouble him with another Packet[2] which he will be so good as to consecrate[3] at his Leisure. That he may continue to enjoy his happy flow of spirits, and proceed through Life with a flowing sail of Prosperity and Reputation is the wish, and the Hope, and the confident Expectation of his much obliged humble servt.,

T! Smollett

Address: Not available. *Source:* MS. in BM. *First Printing:* in 1769, along with Letters 58 and 59. See Letter 58.

[1] In this last letter of the correspondence between Smollett and Wilkes, Smollett seems to have wished to maintain his friendship with Wilkes despite their increasing political differences, soon to erupt into the violent conflict found in the pages of Smollett's *Briton* and Wilkes' *North Briton.* In this conflict Wilkes was the first to indulge in personal insults.

[2] The contents of this packet are unknown. Noyes (p. 200) suggested that it may have contained pamphlets opposing Wilkes' anonymously printed *Observations on the Papers Relative to the Rupture with Spain, laid before both Houses of Parliament on Friday, Jan. 29th, 1762,* published 9 Mar. 1762. This was an apology on behalf of Pitt, who had recently resigned from his office of Prime Minister.

[3] In this context what Smollett meant by *consecrate* is uncertain. Perhaps the statement was ironical.

(104)

Letter 85

To John Moore

Chelsea, April 10, 1762

Dear Sir,

Tho' our Correspondence has suffered a long Interruption, I take it for granted that our mutual Regard is not at all impaired. In this opinion, I take the Liberty to introduce to your acquaintance and good offices the Bearer, Mr. Holt,[1] and his two Pupils, Messrs. Ancre.[2] The Governour[3] is a native of Denmark, and the two young Gentlemen are sons of a rich merchant in Norway. They are travelling for Improvement, and tho' I have not the Pleasure of knowing them personally, a particular friend of mine has described their Characters in such a favourable point of view that I will venture to recommend them as strangers of worth peculiarly entitled to the Rites of Hospitality. Pray, remember me to Dr. Stevenson,[4] Messrs. Barclay,[5] Urie,[6] and all my other Glasgow Friends, and allow me to be still

Your very affectionate Friend and Servt.,
T. Smollett

Address: Not available. *Source:* MS. of PTS. *First Printing:* Noyes, 73–4.

Letter 86

To John Moore

Chelsea June 1, 1762

Dear Sir,

I was lately favoured with yours by the hands of Mr. Richardson[7] whom, however, I had not the good Fortune to see. The Long Interruption in our Correspondence had made no alteration in my Friendship, nor did I suppose it had an Effect upon yours, as you

---

[1] Unidentified.

[2] It is difficult to be certain whether Smollett wrote *Ancre* or *Anere*. In either case, the young students are not yet identified.

[3] Tutor.　　　　　　　　　　　　　　　　[4] See Letter 29, n. 1, p. 47.

[5] See Letter 2, n. 6, p. 1.　　　　　　　　[6] See Letter 20, n. 4, p. 32.

[7] Possibly William Richardson (1743–1814), who became in 1772 Professor of Humanity at the University of Glasgow. For his editing of Smollett's *Ode to Independence*, published in 1773, see his *The Maid of Lochlin: A Lyrical Drama. with Legendary Odes, and Other Poems* (London, 1801), 121–3.

are probably convinced by this time from a Letter of Introduction I some time ago wrote you in favour of some Gentlemen from Norway,[1] who propose to make the Tour of Scotland.

I am much affected by your kind Concern for my Health, and believe the Remedy you propose[2] might have a happy Effect, but it must be postponed. To tell you the Truth, I have a Presentiment that I shall never see Scotland again.[3] Be that as it may, I shall ever retain for it a Regard which is truly filial.

I have had no attack of the Asthma these two months, but I am extremely emaciated, and am afflicted with a tickling Catarrh, and cough all night without ceasing. My appetite holds good; my spirits are tolerable; and I believe I might retrieve my Constitution by a determined Course of Exercise and the Cold Bath.[4] But neither my Indolence nor my occupation will permit me to persevere in these Endeavours.

I am happy in the good opinion of Mrs. Moore, but should be still more happy, had I the opportunity of cultivating it in person.[5] I beg you will present her with my best Respects and most cordial affection.

If any of my old Friends in Glasgow remember me, let them know I still review our Connections with intermingled Pleasure and Regret. When you have an idle hour, you cannot employ it more charitably than in writing to

Your affectionate Friend and very humble Servt.,

T⸳ Smollett

Mr. Richardson left a Card of Direction at my House, but, with respect to returning Visits, I must plead the Privilege of broken Health, and a severity of indispensible Engagements that will not allow me to observe these Punctilios.[6] I return no Visits. I frequent no Company, but live sequestered in this Corner like an Owl in an Ivy Bush.[7]

[1] See Letter 85.

[2] This remedy is not mentioned in Dr. John Moore's life of Smollett in the first volume of Moore's edition of Smollett's *Works*.

[3] Smollett visited Scotland in 1766.

[4] Smollett always advocated exercise, cold bathing, and plunging into the ocean (Letter 94).

[5] Smollett saw Mrs. Moore in 1766.   [6] Petty formalities.

[7] This simile is found in Jonathan Swift's *Polite Conversation*, Dialogue I. See *The Works of Dr. Jonathan Swift*. 8 vols. (Edinburgh and Glasgow, 1756), vii, 303–4: 'Ld Sparkish . . . pr'ythee how did the fool look? *Col.* Look! egad, he look'd for all the world like an owl in an ivy-bush.' For the popular meaning of this simile, one which both Swift and Smollett may have had in mind, see *Ivy Bush* in Francis Grose's *Classical Dictionary of the Vulgar Tongue*, where it is explained as 'a simile for a meagre or weasel-faced man, with a large wig, or bushy hair'.

Address: To Mr. John Moore Surgeon at Glasgow North Britain. Beneath
the address is the following: 'Free John Wilkes', in the handwriting of
John Wilkes, which appears to be a frank. See postscript of Letter 43.
Source: MS. of PTS. *First Printing:* Partly by Irving, 20. A more complete text in Noyes, 75–6 lacks the postscript.

Letter 87

To John Moore

Chelsea, Augt. 19, 1762

Dear Sir,

Your last found me in the Country[1] to which I had repaired for
the Benefit of a purer Air; but whether it was too keen for my
Lungs, or the change of Bed produced a fresh Cold, I was driven
home by the Asthma; and soon after I went to Dover with a View
to bathe in the Sea, and to use the Exercise of riding on Horseback,[2]
and sailing in a Vessel alternately. There too I was disappointed.
Immediately after my Arrival, the weather broke, my asthma returned, my flesh fell away, and my spirits failed so that I returned
very disconcolate, and almost despairing of Relief. The Journey,
however, did me Service. I have been at home these Eight Days,
and find myself better than I have been these three years. Indeed, I
am at present perfectly well, but how long I shall enjoy this Respite
I cannot foresee. The Civilities you have shewn to the three
Foreigners[3] on my account I shall never forget. They are very full
of your Praise, and talk much of the Hospitality and Industry of the
People of Glasgow. I am much obliged to you for your kind Expressions of Concern about my Health and Fortune. With respect
to the last, I have no Cause to complain of want of Encouragement.
The Public has been always a liberal Patron to me since I commenced Author. My Difficulties have arisen from my own Indiscretion; from a warm temper easily provoked to Rashness; from a
want of Courage to refuse what I could not grant without doing
Injustice to my own Family; from Indolence, Bashfullness, and
want of Oeconomy. I am sensible of all my Weaknesses. I have
suffered by them severely, but I have not Vigour of mind sufficient to reform and so I must go on at the old rate to the End of
the Chapter.

[1] Where Smollett stayed in the country at this time is unknown.

[2] In Letter 86 (to John Moore), Smollett had hoped to improve his health by
'Exercise and the Cold Bath'.

[3] See Letter 85, in which Smollett asked Moore to entertain two young
gentlemen, sons of a wealthy merchant of Norway.

To John Moore, 19 August 1762

Your Conjecture is right in supposing I still write some articles in the Critical Review. As I am Proprietor[1] of that work, I should be a Fool to give it up at a Time when it begins to indemnify me for all the Vexation and Loss[2] I have sustained by it; but the Laborious Part of Authorship I have long resigned. My Constitution will no longer allow me to toil as formerly. I am now so thin you would hardly know me. My Face is shrivelled up by the asthma like an ill dried Pippin, and my Legs are as thick at the Ancle as at the Calf. If we have a Peace this Season, and I live till the Spring, I will endeavour to manage Matters so as to be able to make an Excursion to the South of France.[3] I made a Push to go Physician to our Army in Portugal, but miscarried. The Secretary of war[4] professed great Friendship and assured me I might command his best offices. I asked the Place. He expressed great Concern that I had not applied a week before. He said both the Physicians were appointed. This was true, but two other Physicians have been appointed since. You see how much I may depend upon the Friendship of this Gentleman. If my Health had held out, I would have buffeted the storms of Life without having Recourse to the Protection of any man. As it is, I hope no misfortune shall ever be able to tame the Freeborn spirit of,

> Dear Sir, Your affectionate humble Servt.,
> T⁙ Smollett

I offer my best Respects to Mrs. Moore.

Address: To Mr. John Moore Surgeon at Glasgow North Britain. *Source:* MS. at UEL. *First Printing: The New Scots Magazine*, ii (1829), 406–7. See also this letter edited by Noyes in *MLN*, xlii (1927), 231–5.

[1] Just when Smollett became a proprietor, or the sole proprietor of the *Critical Review* is not known, though it is almost certain that he was the principal editor of this important periodical review from its beginning in 1756.

[2] Smollett was violently attacked many times because of what were assumed to be his reviews in the *Critical Review* (Letter 75, n. 3, p. 95). It is quite possible that from 1756 to 1762 Smollett lost money in maintaining the publication of the *Critical Review*. For data on this point, see Knapp, 179–82.

[3] In June 1763, Smollett travelled to Nice, where he lived until his return to England in July 1765.

[4] Charles Townshend (1725–1767). For brief accounts of him, including Smollett's, see Edward S. Noyes, 'Another Smollett Letter', *MLN*, xlii (1927), 234–5; and Smollett's *Humphry Clinker*, ed. Knapp (Oxford University Press, 1966), 114 and 362.

Letter 88
To Dr. William Hunter

Bath, Octr. 2, 1762

Dear Sir,

I am much affected by the last Mark of your Friendship[1] which I received the day before I set out on my Journey, and hope you will give me leave to enjoy it in my own way.

I have been at Southampton and crossed the Country from the new Forrest to Bath[2] where I am now settled in private Lodgings. My Health was so indifferent during the whole Journey that I was obliged to get out of Bed every night and sit two hours untill the Difficulty of Breathing abated. Since my arrival in Bath I have, in spite of a fresh Cold, slept very well, without any Interruption from the asthma. I drink moderately of the water, ride out every day on the Downs, eat like a Horse, and if I could recover a little Flesh I should think myself already cured; but the Truth is I am thinner than when I last saw you, and begin to be afraid of looking in the Glass of a morning. I believe my breathing so easily is owing to the warmth and moisture of the air at Bath, which seems to be peculiarly adapted to my Lungs. Yet I can feel a very sensible Effect from the waters. I have no sooner drank a large Glass of them hot from the Pump than my Face, my Hands, and Feet begin to glow; and this Sensation is succeeded by an itching and tingling all over the Surface of my Body, resembling what is called the prickly Heat in the west indies. I think I can plainly percieve these mineral waters opening up the obstructed Capillaries, and restoring the Perspiration which in the Extremities had been in a great measure lost. I

[1] Smollett's promissory note, a part of this letter, but dated 21 Sept. 1762, shows that he had recently received fifty pounds, which he assumed to be a loan, from his distinguished friend, Dr. William Hunter. Hunter preserved this letter and added the following some years later in his own handwriting:

London, 13th May, 1766

In case of my death I desire my Executors will not make any demand upon Dr. Smollet, because I sent the money to him as a present, never meaning to take it again.

William Hunter

This is pleasant evidence of Hunter's generosity, and of his very friendly relations with Smollett.

[2] This is all that is known about this journey of Smollett. On his way to Southampton it is likely that again he visited at Headly Park, Hampshire the relatives of his friend, William Huggins, who had died in 1761. From the New Forest, near Southampton, to Bath was of course a very attractive route in autumn, which Smollett must have enjoyed in spite of his miserable health.

intend in a few days to bathe with a View to open still more effectually the Strainer of the skin. I beg pardon for taking up so much of your time, but the Subject is interesting to,

(Dear Doctor,)
Your much obliged and affectionate humble Servt.,
T: Smollett

My Compts. to our friends Dr. Macaulay[1] and Pitcairn[2]

London, Septr. 21, 1762
I promise to pay to Doctor Wm. Hunter or order on Demand the Sum of Fifty Pounds value recieved of him by me
T: Smollett

£50..00.0

Address: Not available. *Source:* MS. in RCS. *First Printing:* Extract published by Victor Plarr in *British Medical Journal,* ii (1904), 1096. See also Noyes, 77–8, and 202–3.

Letter 89

To John Home[3]

Chelsea, Decr. 27, 1762
Dear Sir,
My Flesh continues to waste, and I begin to think the best chance I have for Recovering will be a Removal into a warmer climate. As I am unwilling to eat the Bread of Idleness, and flatter myself that I might be still in some shape serviceable to my Country, I cannot help expressing my wish that, instead of the Pension,[4] I were

---

[1] See Letter 17, n. 1, p. 27.   [2] See Letter 10, n. 4, p. 15.

[3] See Letter 6, n. 6, p. 10. John Home, who was in 1762 a private secretary to the Earl of Bute, had known Smollett since 1749. About that time he wrote to Alexander Carlyle: 'Your friend Smollett, who has a thousand good, nay, the best qualities, and whom I love more than he thinks I do, has got on Sunday last three hundred pounds for his *Mask.*' (The *Mask* was Smollett's *Alceste*). For the quoted sentence see Henry MacKenzie's *The Works of John Home,* 3 vols. (Edinburgh, 1822), i, 137. For additional data concerning the relations between Smollett and Home, see Noyes, 204, and Knapp, *passim.*

[4] Smollett may have applied for a pension, or was promised one as a reward for his *Briton* (May 1762–Feb. 1763), written in support of the Earl of Bute's administration, but he never received one.

gratified with some moderate Consulship abroad, the salary of which would enable me to live with Comfort. In the last ministry I made some advances towards the Consulship of Madrid[1] for which I thought myself in some respects qualified, as I understood the Spanish Language and was personally known to Mr. Wall, the minister of his catholic majesty.[2] But this Place was thought ~~too~~ [*sic*] far above my Pretensions. I was, however, offered the Consulate of Nice in Italy,[3] the appointments[4] of which were not sufficient to maintain my Family, and even those depended upon the war. I understand that there is in time of Peace an English Consul at Marseilles with a very moderate Salary, and that the place is now vacant. The Climate of that Country, would, I am persuaded, suit with my Constitution, and should I be thought unworthy of filling the office at Madrid, which is also vacant, perhaps the Earl ⟨of Bute⟩[5] would, upon a Representation of my Case, indulge me with the Consulship of Marseilles.[6]

I need say no more upon the Subject but that if you think there is the least Presumption, or Impropriety in making such a Request, you will take no further notice of this Hint, but suppress it as an Indiscretion of,

Dear Sir,

Your much obliged Servt.,

T�: Smollett

Address: To John Home Esqr. at his Lodgings in Chapel Court South Audley Street. *Source:* MS. in HCSNJ. *First Printing:* Noyes, 78–9.

[1] See Letter 65, n. 4, p. 83.

[2] Richard Wall (1694–1778), born in Ireland, was Lieutenant-General of the armies in Spain in 1755, and also a prominent international diplomat. Spanish ambassador in London from 1748 to 1752. With his permission, Smollett inscribed to him (to Don Ricardo Wall) his translation of *Don Quixote* in 1755 For an account of Wall's diplomatic activities, see Smollett's *The Continuation of the Complete History of England*, i (1760), 86, 232, and 276; and iv (1761), 351.

[3] Though Smollett did not accept this offer, he tried in vain later to obtain the consulship at Nice and also at Leghorn (Noyes, 205; and Knapp, 271–2).

[4] The money paid to a public officer.

[5] The words *of Bute* were erased, perhaps by Smollett (Noyes, 205).

[6] Smollett did not receive this consulship in spite of his support of the Earl of Bute. See n. 4, p. 110.

Letter 90
To Richard Smith Esq.[1] of New Jersey, North America

London, May 8, 1763

I am favoured with yours of the 26th of February,[2] and cannot but be pleased to find myself as a Writer so high in your Esteem. The Curiosity you express with regard to the Particulars of my Life and the variety of situations in which I may have been cannot be gratified within the Compass of a Letter. Besides, there are some Particulars of my Life which it would ill become me to relate.[3] The only Similitude between the Circumstances of my own Fortune and those I have attributed to Roderick Random consists in my being born of a reputable Family in Scotland, in my being bred a Surgeon, and having served as a Surgeon's mate on board a man of war during the Expedition to Carthagene. The low Situations in which I have exhibited Roderick I never experienced in my own Person. I married, very young, a native of Jamaica, a young Lady well known and universally respected under the name of Miss Nancy Lassells,[4] and by her I enjoy a comfortable tho' moderate Estate in that Island. I practised Surgery in London after having improved myself by travelling in France and other forreign Countries,[5] 'till the year 1749, when I took my Degree of Doctor in Medicine,[6] and have lived ever since in Chelsea, (I hope) with credit and Reputation. No man knows better than Mr. Rivington[7] what Time I employed in writing the four first Volumes of the History of England; and indeed the short Period in which that work was finished appears almost incredible to myself, when I recollect that I turned over and consulted above three hundred Volumes in the Course of my Labour. Mr. Rivington likewise knows that I spent

[1] Richard Smith (1735–1803) was Recorder of Burlington, New Jersey, provincial councilor-at-law for that State, and a member of the Continental Congress, from which he resigned in 1776. A Quaker, he was recognized as a man of wide learning and integrity.

[2] Richard Smith's letter, expressing great admiration for Smollett's novels and his *History of England* is in print. See Knapp, 'Smollett's Admirers in Eighteenth-Century America', in *Williams [College] Alumni Review*, Williamstown, Massachusetts, xxii (1929), 114–15.

[3] It is futile to speculate about these 'particulars'.

[4] Ann Lassells. See Knapp, 38, 39, 41–2. See also Knapp, 'Ann Smollett, Wife of Tobias Smollett', *PMLA*, xlv (1930), 1035–49.

[5] Concerning Smollett's travels in France and other areas in Europe before 1750 very little information is available.

[6] The exact month when Smollett received his M.D. from Marischal College, Aberdeen, Scotland, is uncertain (Knapp, 49, 144).

[7] James Rivington, publisher (Letter 28, n. 1, p. 45).

the best part of a year in revising, correcting, and improving the Quarto Edition which is now going to Press and will be continued in the same Size to the late Peace. Whatever Reputation I may have got by this work has been dearly bought by the Loss of Health, which I am of opinion I shall never retrieve. I am now going to the South of France[1] in order to try the Effects of that climate, and very probably I shall never return. I am much obliged to you for the Hope you express that I have obtained some Provision from his majesty, but the Truth is I have neither Pension nor Place, nor am I of that Disposition which can stoop to Sollicit either.[2] I have always piqued myself upon my Independancy, and I trust in God I shall preserve it to my dying day. Exclusive of some small detached Performances that have been published occasionally in Papers and Magazines, the following is a genuine List of my Productions.[3] Roderick Random. The Regicide, a Tragedy. A Translation of Gil Blas. A Translation of Don Quixote. An Essay upon the external use of water. Peregrine Pickle. Ferdinand Count Fathom. Great Part of the Critical Review.[4] A very small part of a Compendium of Voyages. The complete History of England, and Continuation. A Small Part of the modern Universal History. Some Pieces in the British Magazine, comprehending the whole of Sir Launcelot Greaves. A small part of the Translation of Voltaire's works, including all the notes historical and critical to be found in that Translation. I am much mortified to find it is believed in America that I have lent my name to Booksellers; that is a species of Prostitution of which I am altogether incapable. I had engaged with Mr. Rivington, and made some Progress in a work exhibiting the present state of the world,[5] which work I shall finish if I recover my Health. If you should see Mr. Rivington, please give my kindest Compts. to him, tell him I wish him all manner of Happiness, tho' I have little to expect for my own share, having lost my only child,[6]

[1] Smollett left for France about the middle of June 1763.

[2] Although Smollett had applied for various consulships, he had always maintained an independent spirit, of which he was proud.

[3] Smollett's list of his productions prior to 1763 is surprisingly incomplete: he omits his early poem, 'The Tears of Scotland'; his early satires, *Advice*, and *Reproof*; his comedy, *The Reprisal*; and the *Briton*.

[4] To the first fourteen volumes of the *Critical Review* (1756–62), Smollett must have made a tremendous contribution.

[5] *The Present State of All Nations*, Compiled or edited by Smollett, 8 vols., (London, 1768–9).

[6] Elizabeth Smollett died 3 Apr. 1763, aged fifteen. About 1758 she probably attended a school for girls in Chelsea kept by a Mrs. Aylesworth and Madame Beete. Upon Smollett's recommendation of this school, Wilkes sent his daughter Polly there. There is a tradition that Elizabeth wrote poetry. See Knapp. 'Elizabeth Smollett, Daughter of Tobias Smollett', *RES*, viii (1932), 312–15.

a fine Girl of Fifteen, whose Death has overwhelmed myself and my wife with unutterable Sorrow.

I have now complied with your Request, and beg in my turn you will commend me to all my Friends in America. I have endeavoured more then once to do the Colonies some service,[1] and I am,

Sir,

Your very humble Servt.,

T.ˢ Smollett

Address: Not available. *Source:* MS. in HSP. *First Printing: The Port Folio* (Philadelphia, 7 Feb. 1801).

Letter 91

To Dr. William Hunter

Jermyn Street,[2] June 14, 1763

Dear Doctor,

In case I should not have the Pleasure of taking my Leave of you by word of mouth, I seize this opportunity of thanking you for the manifold Instances of your Friendship which I have received, Instances which I shall ever remember with the strongest Emotions of Gratitude, Esteem and affection. Should I never return, I hope I shall leave Effects sufficient to discharge all the Debts I have contracted. I am now ambitious of nothing so much as of dying with the Character of an honest man. Such is the Tenderness of my nature enervated by ill Health and misfortune that I cannot well stand the shock of parting from my best Friends. Pray tell my dear friend Dr. Macaulay[3] that I shall write to him as soon as I arrive at Boulogne. I intended to have left with him a power of Attorney to transact some of my affairs, but his being taken ill prevented me from conferring with him upon that Subject so that I have left a Power with Mr. Hamilton,[4] and will explain this affair in my Letter to the Doctor. I heartily pray God you may proceed in the Path you are in to wealth and Honour,[5] that you may enjoy every species of Happiness, and continue to do Honour to your Country, as well as

---

[1] For one eloquent example of Smollett's praise of the British colonists of America, see his *Complete History of England,* iv (1758), 660–1.

[2] It is likely that Smollett found that Dr. Hunter was not at his home in Jermyn Street, and that instead of seeing him he wrote and left this farewell letter. See Noyes, 208.

[3] Dr. George Macaulay. See Letter 17, n. 1, p. 27.

[4] See Letter 51, n. 4, p. 67.

[5] Smollett's prayers for his close friend were all granted.

to your particular Friends, in the number of whom, I flatter myself you will admit,

Dear Sir,
Your much obliged humble servt.,
T⁹ Smollett

I cannot help expressing an eager Desire that your Brother's future Conduct may intitle him to a revival of those favourable sentiments in you, which he has indiscreetly forfeited.

Address: Not available. *Source:* MS. in RCS. *First Printing:* Extract published by Victor Plarr in *British Medical Journal*, ii (1904), 1096; Noyes, 83–4.

Letter 92

To Dr. William Hunter

Boulogne sur mer, chez Mons. Bouvier[1]
July 11, 1763

Dear Sir,

It is no great Compliment to write you a Letter when I have nothing else to do, and yet it is a Duty which I should take pleasure in doing were I employed in the utmost Hurry of occupation.

I have been out of order 'this Fortnight with a severe cold which has handled me severely, and reduced me so much that I now perceive the State of my Health becomes a very serious affair. I have nothing for it but a Journey to the South, which is likely to be retarded by an Incident equally troublesome and unexpected. My Books[2] are stopped at the Custom House of Boulogne on pretence that they must be sent to Amiens in order to be examined by the *Chambre Syndicale* lest they should contain something to the Prejudice of the state, and of the Catholic Religion. I have taken the Liberty to write to the Earl of Hertford[3] as British Ambassador

---

[1] In Smollett's *Travels*, Letters II and III, Mr. Bouvier is referred to as 'Mr. B——', his landlord in Boulogne.

[2] For the list of books which Smollett took to France, see A. C. Hunter, 'Les Livres De Smollett Détenus Par La Douane à Boulogne en 1763', in *Revue de Littérature Comparée*, xi (1931), 763–7. This list is reprinted in Knapp, 249. Concerning further information about the detention of Smollett's books, see Eugène Joliat, *Smollett Et La France* (Paris, 1935), 249–53, and Smollett's *Travels*, Letters II and III.

[3] Francis Seymour-Conway (1718–94), first Earl of Hertford, Earl of Yarmouth, and first Marquis of Hertford, Ambassador to France, 1763–5.

at Paris, intreating his Lordship to interpose with the french ministry that my Books may be restored. I think myself as a British subject intitled to his Lordship's Protection. I have likewise writt to my Cousin, the Dutchess of Douglas,[1] begging her to reinforce my Request with the Ambassador, but what Effect my Letters of application will have I cannot guess. I am afraid I shall lose all the Books, a Loss which I shall feel in many respects. For, I can neither write the Preface to the modern Universal History, nor finish the Continuation of my own History of England, without having the Books before me. Besides, my poor wife who does not understand much French will have no sort of literary Amusement.[2]

My friend Dr. Macaulay[3] has been informed that the lower Town of Boulogne where I lodge is worse than Wappping.[4] He has been much misinformed. The lower Town is much more pleasant than the upper Town. The streets are broad and clean and well paved, and the Houses very commodious. I would never desire to live in a more agreable Place if my Health did not require a milder Climate. As for Company, I have none; but I have sometime ago learned to live at home, and if I was well, I should be entertained by the Humours and Characters of the french People.

I am now determined at all Events to travel by Land to Nice in Provence, where, I am told, the cheapness of Living will in a little time make amends for the extraordinary Expence of the Journey; and I expect great Benefit to my Health from travelling seven hundred miles by Land, as well as pleasure in viewing the finest Country in the Universe.

If I can be of any Service to you in the way of picking up Books[5] either at Paris, or Lyons, or Marseilles, I hope you will tell me that I

---

[1] Margaret, eldest daughter of James Douglas of Mains, Dumbartonshire, married, in 1758, Archibald Hamilton, Duke of Douglas. In the summer of 1763 she was in Paris in connection with the famous Douglas Cause, and Smollett visited her *en route* to Nice. Why Smollett referred to her as his cousin (a distant cousin) is due probably to the fact that the second wife of Smollett's grandfather, Sir James Smollett, was Elizabeth Hamilton, perhaps related to the Duke of Douglas. For an excellent account of the Duchess of Douglas, and her portrait, see Lillian de la Torre, *The Heir of Douglas* (New York, 1952), 172, and *passim*.

[2] Among Smollett's books conveyed to France were the works of Shakespeare, and the comedies of Congreve.

[3] Dr. George Macaulay (Letter 17, n. 1, p. 27).

[4] This statement is found also in Smollett's *Travels*, Letter III.

[5] Dr. William Hunter was an avid book collector. At a book-auction in Paris in 1769, he was reported to have spent 1,000 guineas. See the *Whitehall Evening-Post: or, London Intelligencer* (Tues. 15 Aug.–Thurs. 17 Aug. 1769).

may in some measure shew with what Gratitude, affection and Esteem, I am,

Dear Doctor

Your much obliged humble servt.,

T:ˢ Smollett

Address: To Dr. Hunter at his House in Jermyn Street London. *Source:* MS. of Robert Taylor. *First Printing:* By Knapp, *NQ,* (Aug. 1960), 299–300.

Letter 93

To Alexander Reid[1]

Boulogne, Augt. 3, 1763

Dear Sir,

Your obliging Letter was doubly acceptable, both for the Entertainment I received from it, and as it convinced me that I am still remembred with regard by my old Friends in Chelsea. Indeed I cannot help respecting Chelsea as a second native Place, notwithstanding the irreparable Misfortunes which happened to me while I resided in it. I mean the Loss of my Health, and of that which was dearer to me than Health itself, my darling Child,[2] whom I cannot yet remember with any degree of Composure.

With respect to my Constituion, I have lost ground since I left England. I now bathe in the Sea, and shall in ten days or a Fortnight set out for Nice in Provence, a Journey of Eight hundred and sixty-four miles. This is my last Stake, and if it does not answer, I must give up all thoughts of ever seeing my Friends in England. When there is no Remedy we must submit. Before I arrived in France I thought the climate of England was the most dissagreable on the face of the Earth, but here it is a thousand times more vexatious, more variable, and more inclement.

I am very glad to hear your Concert[3] was so brilliant, and I hope

---

[1] Alexander Reid (1719–89), Assistant Surgeon for forty-eight years at the Royal Hospital in Chelsea. His *Consultations on most of the Disorders That require the Assistance of Surgery,* translated from the French of Le Dran, was published in 1766. Reid was a specialist in inoculation for smallpox. He became in 1759 a member of the Sublime Society of Beef Steaks, and was also active in other social groups, including the Bowling Green Society of Chelsea. See Thomas Faulkner, *An Historical and Topographical Description of Chelsea and its Environs,* 2 vols., (Chelsea, 1829), ii, 280–2.

[2] Elizabeth Smollett (Letter 90, n. 6, p. 113).

[3] In Thomas Faulkner (*op cit.,* ii, 281), there is an allusion to The Ladies' Morning Musical Meeting, a society active in 1770, and of which Reid was the steward.

(117)

all your Chelsea Societies will continue to flourish. I understand there is a Lodge of french free masons at Boulogne,[1] but I am not well enough to visit them. I am much mortified that my ill Health will not permit me to enjoy a Bottle of good Claret which I have at the Rate of Fifteen pence sterling. In Languedoc I can have it for the fifteenth part of that sum. The season here is very backward. Green Geese,[2] Soles and Turbot are just come in; there is not an Apri[c]ock ripe within three Leagues of Boulogne. However, the Rye Harvest is begun, and in ten days they will cut down their wheat. Every thing here is done in a clumsy and slovenly manner, which is very dissagreable and even shocking to those who have been accustomed to English neatness; and there is a total want of Delicacy in the manners of the People. They are generally civil, but they have no Sentiment, and their Ignorance and Superstition put me out of all patience.

My wife who enjoys pretty good Health joins me in my best respects to Mrs. Reid, and in best Wishes for your Children, who are ~~have~~ [*sic*] by this time, I hope, quite recovered of the Hooping Cough. I pray God they may live to be a Comfort to you both, and that you may never feel the Pangs of that unspeakable Grief which the Loss of a beloved child inspires.

Pray, remember me to my good Friends Messrs. Wilton[3] and Russel,[4] and to all our Brotherhood at the Swan.[5] When you see Halford,[6] tell him I am surprised he never answered my Letter; and believe me to be with great Truth and affection,

Dear Sawney,

Your sincere friend and humble Servt.,

T: Smollett

Address: To Mr. Alexr. Reid Surgeon in Chelsea by London. *Source:* MS. in HU. *First Printing:* Thomas Faulkner, *An Historical and Topographical Description of Chelsea, and its Environs*, 2 vols. (Chelsea, 1829), i, 271–2.

[1] See note 5.   [2] Young geese, or goslings.

[3] Perhaps John Wilton, Deputy Treasurer of Chelsea in 1755.

[4] Alexander Russell, M.D. (1715–68), physician at St. Thomas's Hospital. See *DNB.*

[5] In Smollett's time the Old Swan Tavern stood on the banks of the Thames not far from Paradise Row. It is likely that it was the meeting-place of a Masonic lodge, and it is practically certain that Smollett was a Freemason while in Chelsea.

[6] Perhaps Oakley Halford, who resided after 1748 in Cheyne Walk, Chelsea. See Walter H. Godfrey, *Survey of London*, vol. ii, Part I, Chelsea, (London, *c.* 1909), 36.

Letter 94
To Dr. [? William] Hunter

Boulogne sur mer, Augt. 11, 1763

Dear Sir,

Two or three Posts ago, I took the Liberty to write a Letter to the Earl of Hertford[1] in order to express my acknowledgement for the Trouble his Lordship had taken in the affair of my Books; and I gave him to understand that I had heard nothing of them since his Lordship had been so good as to recommend them to the attention of Mr. Neville at Paris.

Yesterday they were delivered to me unexamined in consequence of an order sent to the Intendant of Picardy; and this day I have written a Letter of Thanks to Mr. Neville,[2] but as Lord Hertford may from his peculiar Benevolence of Disposition take the Trouble of writing again to Mr. Neville on this subject, and I am unwilling to trouble his Lordship with a third Letter, I shall take it as a very singular Favour if you will present my most respectfull Compliments to him, and let him know that the Books are restored. This Request I am the more encouraged to make as I know you are often at his Lordship's House.

I received your obliging Letter in due Course, and the Contents of it are engraven on my Heart.

This is the twentieth day of my bathing in the sea from which I have received such Benefit as almost transcends Belief.

A few days ago, I dined with General Paterson,[3] late Governour of Nice, who treated me with the most cordial Kindness, and favoured me with such Recommendations and Directions as will equally redound to my Honour and Satisfaction.

You say you should be glad to have every curious Book on the face of the Earth; but I should be afraid of sending you some Books which you may have already.

I propose to set out for Paris in a Fortnight on my way to Lyons,

---

[1] See Letter 92, n. 3, p. 115.

[2] Richard Neville Aldworth Neville (1717–93) was acting as Minister Plenipotentiary when Lord Hertford arrived as ambassador from England in 1763.

[3] Sir James Paterson (?–1765) of Bannockburn, Scotland. He had been a Lieutenant-General in the army of the King of Sardinia, and a governor of Nice. See *Scots Magazine*, xxvii (1765), 502, for his obituary. For Smollett's later tributes to Paterson, see *Travels Through France and Italy*, Letters 3 and 14.

but wheresoever I may be, I shall never forget that I am with the most perfect Friendship and Esteem,

Dear Doctor,

Your much obliged humble servt.,

T⁵ Smollett

Address: Not available. *Source:* MS. at HCSNJ. *First Printing:* Noyes, 86–8.

Letter 95

To Dr. William Hunter

Nice, Feby. 6, 1764

Dear Sir,

I received your last Favour at Boulogne, when I was upon the Wing to the southward, and deferred answering it untill I should be able to say something satisfactory of the Place where I might pass the winter. I was induced to visit Montpellier by sundry Considerations, tho' it is about twelve Leagues out of the Road to Nice. I expected my Baggage at Cette, which is the Port of Montpellier. I wished to see the antiquities of Nismes,[1] which gave me incredible Pleasure; and I hoped that the Air of Montpellier would agree with my Constitution so as to save me the Trouble and Expence of a long Journey to the Banks of the Var.[2] I found the Place very agreable, and met with some Families of English People with whom I could have passed my Time in a very sociable way; but in a few days after I arrived, the weather broke up; it rained incessantly a whole week; and this change of the Atmosphere relaxed me to such a degree that all my complaints returned together with a most uncomfortable Dejection of spirits. I had the advice of one Dr. Fitzmorrice,[3] and honest irish Physician of the Place; and I consulted Dr. Fizes,[4] the Boerhaave[5] of Montpellier,

[1] For Smollett's reaction to Nismes (Nîmes), see his *Travels Through France and Italy*, Letter X. For the relations between Smollett's personal letters and his *Travels*, see Kahrl, Ch. VIII. See also Martz, 68–72.

[2] The river Var flows into the Mediterranean a few miles west of Nice. For Smollett's description of this river, see his *Travels*, Letter XII.

[3] Unidentified. In Smollett's *Travels* (first edition, 1766) Letter XI (Montpellier, November 12) is the following: 'I was favoured with the advice of Dr. Fitz-Maurice, a very worthy sensible physician, settled in this place.'

[4] For Smollett's detailed account of his consultation with Dr. Fizès, see his *Travels*, Letter XI.

[5] Herman Boerhaave (1668–1738), a celebrated Dutch physician, of whom a short biography was written in 1739 by Dr. Samuel Johnson.

(120)

TOBIAS SMOLLETT, *c.* 1764
By Nathaniel Dance

who is an old sordid Scoundrel, and an old woman into the Bargain. I sent him my Case in Latin, which he answered in French. The Correspondence between us was diverting enough. If ever I return to England, you shall see the original Papers.[1] Tho' I expressly assured him that I never discharged any thing like matter from the Lungs, he insisted upon it that I had Tubercules which were suppurated.[2] He prescribed Bouillons of Land Tortoise for a fortnight, opiates at night, and then a Course of Goats milk; but not a word of Exercise.[3] I found he had a set of Phrases and Prescriptions which he applied to all Cases indiscriminately, for when I arrived at Nice, Mr. Mayne, an English Gentleman (now dead),[4] shewed me a Paper of Directions written by Fizes in exactly the same words which he had used to me.

Finding the air of Montpellier too sharp for my Constitution, and the Place too expensive for my Finnances, I set out for Nice on the thirteenth of November, and here I arrived on the twenty-third. As I take it for granted you have seen my Letter to Dr. Macaulay,[5] I need not repeat what I have said to him with respect to my Situation. I have now resided above two months in the place, and find myself surprisingly recovered as to the asthmatic Disorder, the little hectic Fever, and lowness of spirits. All these are gone. I eat heartily. I sleep sound, almost without interruption from the Cough which is much diminished, as well as the spitting, but still the Tuber continues. I grow thinner and thinner; but I am not without hope of recruiting in the spring. Indeed, here is Spring and even Summer all the year. Roses, Jonquills, Ranunculas[6] and Anemonies flower all the year; and in about three weeks, the oranges, Lemons, Citrons and Bergamots[7] will begin to be gathered. Nice is a narrow Town wedged in between a high mountain and the River Paglion which washes the walls on one side and falls into the Mediterranean at the Distance of ten yards from the Corner of one of the Bastions. This River at present puts me in mind of a Scotch Brook divided in several small streamlets brawling over a broad Bed of Peebles;[8] but after sudden storms it swells to a very formidable stream; and in the year 1744, many hundreds of the french and spaniards were drowned in it, after having been repulsed

---

[1] These papers are printed in Smollett's *Travels*, Letter XI.

[2] Pus-secreting tubercles.

[3] Smollett expressed in several letters his belief in the value of exercise.

[4] Unidentified. In his *Travels* (Letter XII) Smollett referred to one Mr. M——e whom he had seen at Boulogne and met again when he reached Nice in November, 1763.

[5] A lost letter to Dr. George Macaulay.

[6] The genus of the plant called buttercup.

[7] Pears.   [8] Apparently a misspelling of *pebbles*.

in an attack upon the Piedmontese Intrenchments within a short mile of Nice. The assailants lost five thousand men upon that occasion. The maritime alps begin about a half a mile from the land Gate of Nice, and form a most delightfull amphitheatre extending about a leage [*sic*] all around the City. The mountains are covered with olives to the very tops, and these trees are green all the winter. The Eye is inchanted by a vast Number of white Cassines or Houses rising through the Trees, and each of these Cassines has a Garden with Groves of Oranges and loaded with Fruit. Some of these Houses are magnificent, but the greater part belong to Farmers and Citizens and look much better at a Distance than near at hand. Among them also are two Convents standing in a most imperial situation, and divers old fortified Castles which add greatly to the Beauty of the Prospect. When the wind blows from the mountains (which at a distance are now covered with snow), the air is sharp on the land side of the Town, and I have seen the pools covered with Ice, but on that part of the Rampart which faces the Mediterranean, you enjoy Summer all the year. While the wind blows from the mountains, the weather is always fair because, indeed, there is no room for a collection of Clouds and vapours between the mountains and the sea, and those mountains are so high that the Clouds from Piedmont are detained on the other side. It rains only when the south wind blows the Vapours of the Mediterranean against the Nice side of these mountains; and this is so seldom the Case that we have often clear skies without the least Spot or Blemish for six weeks, two, and even three months successively. Even in the severest weather at Nice, very few People use Fires in their Chambers, and most of the Houses in Town have no Glass in their windows. In such an equal and benign Climate, I apprehend the Perspiration must be equally and happily performed; and to this Cause I chiefly ascribe the free Respiration which I and many other asthmatic people enjoy in this place; for here are some Persons who live comfortably and breathe freely after having found even the Climates of Languedoc and Provence intolerable. At Villa-franca, which is on the other side of the mountain about two miles from hence, the air is still more mild than at Nice because that mountain defends it intirely from the north and East; but then the Place is so confined that there is no room for Exercise. We lie right opposite to Algiers, and (I am told) can see the Island of Corsica when the sky is very clear. Our situation is in the Bottom of a Delightfull Bay within thirty leagues of Marseilles on one hand, and of Genoa on the other; we are at the same distance from Turin. We can go from hence in a Felucca to Leghorn in four and twenty hours; and I own I am strongly tempted to make a short Tour of

To Dr. William Hunter, 6 February 1764

Florence, Rome and Naples, which I think I can finish in one month.[1] With this View I am at present giving my whole attention to the italian Language which I think I shall be able to speak tolerably in six months. All the People of Condition here speak italian, which is used in all Pulpits and in all the Courts of Justice; but the Language of the Country is the old provençal, which is improperly called *Patois*; for *Patois* means no more than the vulgar Dialect of any Language, whereas this is an Original of itself. It is indeed the Language which rose upon the Ruins of the Latin, and was spoke by the Inhabitants of Italy, Spain and France, before each of these nations refined it into the Language which is now spoken in each of those Countries.

If your sister is with you still, pray offer her my most respectfull Compts. and those of my wife, who is in good health and spirits, and sends her best Respects to you also. Remember me kindly to Jock,[2] to Drs. Macaulay,[3] Pitcairn,[4] Dickson,[5] and all my worthy friends; and allow me to be with unalterable Truth, Esteem and affection,

Dear Doctor,
Your much obliged humble servt.,
T⁵ Smollett

Dr. Dr.,

I forgot to mention that the scurvy is not known in this Country; and all the People have the whitest and the soundest Teeth that ever I saw. I wish I could send you a Head,[6] but I am afraid I shall find no opportunity. That there is something in the Climate which attenuates the Blood would appear from the Case of some of our [The remainder of this sentence is completely obliterated by a pen].

Adieu

I went last week to see the Remains of Cemeleon,[7] an old Roman

[1] For Smollett's tour of two months in Italy, see his *Travels*, Letters XXV–XXXV.

[2] John Hunter (1728–93), famous surgeon and anatomist, and brother of Dr. William Hunter.

[3] Dr. George Macaulay (Letter 17, n. 1, p. 27).

[4] See Letter 10, n. 4, p. 15.   [5] See Letter 21, n. 5, p. 36.

[6] Both Dr. William Hunter and his brother John were much interested in anatomical dissection.

[7] For other data on Smollett's visits to this ancient city, see his *Travels*, Letters XIII and XVI. In his *Travels* he referred to the city as Cemenelion, then also called Cimia. For the various spellings of this place, now called Cimiez, and for a picture of the ancient Roman amphitheatre, see John Douglas Errington Loveland, *The Romance of Nice* (London, 1911), Ch. II.

City on a Hill about two miles to the northward of Nice. I found the Ruins of an Amphitheatre which was not large. The Arena is intire, with some of the Steps, and two or three Gateways arched; but the Columns and Façade are intirely destroyed. A great many medals (gold, silver and copper) have been found in the neighbourhood, together with sepulchral and other Inscriptions, and there is an old Temple now converted into a Peasant's House. The Portico is taken away. The arcades are built up with Rubble. The Peasant with his Family of nasty Brats live like so many Rats immediately under the Roof; and the space below serves for a stable, in which I found a starved Ox, a Jack-ass, and a He-goat. I mention this assemblage because in passing thro' Burgundy I saw three Animals of the same species drawing a Plough very peaceable together. Here is no Learning, nor Taste of any kind. All is gothic pride, Ignorance and Superstition.

Address: Not available. *Source:* MS at RCS. *First Printing:* Uncertain. Noyes, 88–94.

Letter 96

To John Moore

London, July 15, 1765

Dear Sir,

I take this opportunity of my friend Mr. Williams[1] to inquire after your Health, and to let you know that I am returned to England after an absence of two years, during which I have been more than once at the Brink of the Grave. After all, I have brought back no more than the skeleton of what I was, but with proper care that skeleton may hang for some few years together. I propose to pass the winter at Bath, and if I find that climate intolerable, I shall once more go into Exile, and never more think of returning. The Bearer, Mr. William, is a very worthy Gentleman, whose son is at your University, boarded with Professor Leechman;[2] I need say no more in the way of Recommendation, knowing how ready you are

---

[1] This Mr. Williams was possibly related to the Rev. W. Williams, curate of Chelsea in 1755. See Thomas Faulkner, *An Historical Description of Chelsea*, 2 vols. (Chelsea, 1829), ii, 87.

[2] William Leechman (1706–85), Professor of Divinity at the University of Glasgow. See *DNB*, and Carlyle, *passim*.

to exercise your Hospitality in favour of all strangers, particularly those who are the Friends of,

Your affectionate humble servt.,
T? Smollett

I live in Brewers Street by Golden Square.[1]

Address: To Mr. John Moore Surgeon in Glasgow. *Source:* M S. of PTS *First Printing:* Partly in Irving, 20. Completely in Noyes, 94–5.

Letter 97

To John Moore

Bath in Somersetshire, Novr. 13, 1765

Dear Sir,

I purposed answering your kind Letter by my old friend Duncan Niven,[2] but he forgot to call on me before his Departure from London, as he promised to do.

Mrs. Williams[3] payed me a Visit on purpose to thank me for the Civilities which she and her Husband recieved from you at Glasgow in consequence of my Recommendation. She seemed very full on the subject and expatiated much on your Politeness and Hospitality. I can do no less than to thank you heartily for your attention to my friends and to protest that nothing would give me more Pleasure than an opportunity to return the obligation to any friend of yours.

Your friendly sollicitude about my Health and concerns requires that I should give you a short sketch of my present situation. I gave up all connection with the Critical Review and every other literary system[4] before I quitted England. Since my return I have writt a few articles merely for amusement;[5] but I have now no concern in the work. The observations I made in the course of my Travels thro' France and Italy I have thrown into a Series of Letters

---

[1] For Brewers Street and Golden Square see Noyes, 215, and Knapp, 258–9.

[2] One of Smollett's important models for his well-known character, Strap, in *Roderick Random*. Duncan Niven (?–1771) was a bailie (magistrate) of Glasgow when he visited Smollett in London in 1765. See Chambers, 53, footnote.

[3] The wife of Mr. Williams referred to in Letter 96.

[4] The other literary productions in which Smollett surely had a part in 1763 were the *British Magazine*, and *The Modern Part* of the *Universal History*.

[5] Unidentified articles which probably appeared in *The Critical Review*, the *British Magazine*, or some other periodical or newspaper. For conjectures about them see Noyes, 215–17.

which will make two Volumes in Octavo. They are now printing, and will be published in the spring.[1] I will not answer for their Success with the Public,[2] but as I have given a sort of natural History of Nice, with my Remarks upon that climate and a Register of the weather, I hope the Performance may be usefull to other valetudinarians who travel for the Recovery of their Health. With respect to my own Health I cannot complain. I have not lately lost any Ground; but, on the contrary, have gained some flesh since my coming to Bath, where I have been these five weeks. I do not, however, flatter myself that I shall continue to mend, for I have always found myself better for about a month after any change of air, and then I relapse into my former state of Invalidity. My Disorder is no other than weak Lungs and a Constitution prone to Catarrhs, with an extraordinary irritability of the nervous System.[3] The Perspiration being stopped by catching cold, what should pass off in that manner is accumulated in the Habit[4] and thrown upon the weakest part of the Viscera, which, in me, happens to be the membrane that lines the Trachea arteria,[5] and the air vesicules. The Glands of these parts are stuffed with the acrimonious matter of the Catarrh; hence a difficulty in breathing, partly from Plenitude, and partly from a spasmodic Constriction, a troublesome Cough, and a Discharge by expectoration, first thin and acrid, and afterwards more bland and digested. My greatest Misfortune is my being so extremely susceptible of cold that I can hardly stir abroad without Danger. The acrimony of my Juices is owing to the Scurvy which has produced a very ugly Eruption on my right hand. Nothing agrees with me so well as hard Exercise, which, however, the Indolence of my Disposition continually counteracts. If I was a Galley slave and kept to hard Labour for two or three years, I believe I should recover my Health intirely. The Bath water agrees with me wonderfully well; and, upon the whole, I am so well at present that some of my friends declare they never saw me look better. But I will venture to say I am not above half as big as I was when you saw me last. To tell you the Truth, I look upon my being alive as a sort of Resuscitation; for last year I thought myself in the last stage of a Consumption. I long eagerly to see you and some other friends in Scotland, but the Distance between us is so great

[1] The *Travels Through France and Italy* were published in London about 8 May 1766, handsomely printed, in two volumes.

[2] For the immediate and very favourable newspaper publicity, reviews, and public reception of the *Travels*, see Noyes, 217, and Knapp, 262–4.

[3] The diagnosis which Smollett sent in Latin to Dr. Fizès contained the following: 'Systema nervosum maxime irritabile.' (*Travels*, Letter XI).

[4] The bodily constitution.

[5] The windpipe.

that I despair of being ever able to gratify my Desire.[1] Make my best Compliments to Mrs. Moore; remember me to all our Glasgow Friends; comfort me with a Letter when you have Leisure time; and believe me to be ever,

Dear Sir,
Your affectionate humble servt.,
T: Smollett

Direct for Dr. Smollett on the South Parade,[2] Bath, Somerset-shire.

Address: To Mr. Moore Surgeon in Glasgow North Britain. *Source:* MS. of PTS. *First Printing:* Partially by Irving, 20. Almost completely by Noyes, 95–7.

Letter 98
To Samuel Mitchelson[3]

Bath, Jany. 3, 1767

Dear Sir,

I am just now favoured with yours and shall with Pleasure comply with your Request in favour of your Nephew, Mr. Anderson, whom I will recommend in the strongest terms to Mr. Campbell at Calcutta,[4] not doubting but he will pay some Regard to my Recommendation, especially as it will be the first Favour I ever asked at his Hands. I must tell you, however, that the last time I heard from him he proposed leaving the East indies sometime next summer so that he may chance to have quitted the Coast before Mr. Anderson arrives.[5] Be that as it may, I am happy in having this opportunity to shew with what Respect and good will I am,

Dear Sir,
Your very humble servt.,
T: Smollett

[1] Smollett was able to go to Glasgow in June 1766.

[2] The South Parade is in the south-east part of Bath near the river Avon, a fashionable urban area two centuries ago.

[3] Samuel Mitchelson (?–1788) of Carrubbers Close, Edinburgh. He was Writer to the Signet and a devotee of music. He probably took Smollett in 1766 to a concert in Saint Cecilia's Hall. In *Humphry Clinker* Bramble's party dined at Mitchelson's (see letter of J. Melford, August 8).

[4] Alexander Campbell, whom Smollett attacked in *Humphry Clinker* (Knapp, 290 ff.).

[5] As Campbell sailed from India on 31 Dec. 1767, he must have received Smollett's letter. What he did to help Mitchelson's nephew is unknown.

To the Duchess of Hamilton

I wish you a happy new year and all manner of Prosperity.

P.S. I have already written the Letter for Mr. Campbell and will send it pr first opportunity.

Address: Not available. *Source:* MS. in BPL. *First Printing:* By Knapp in *NQ*, New Series, iii (1956), 262.

Letter 99
[To the Duchess of Hamilton][1]

Madam,

A severe Indisposition by which I have been confined to my own House these six weeks disables me from taking a Journey to London on purpose to deliver the enclosed and pay my Respects in person.

Thus circumstanced, I beg leave to mention a few Particulars for your Grace's Information touching the Purport[2] of my Nephew's Letter.[3]

The Consulship of Nice is in itself inconsiderable, and only becomes an object of Consequence to me as my bad state of Health obliges me to reside in a warm climate; and I have found by Experience the Air of that country favourable to my Constitution.

I believe no Reversion of any such place is ever granted, and therefore all I could expect is an assurance of being appointed successor to the present Incumbent, should it be my Fate to survive him. The Place is at the Disposal of the Secretary of State for the Southern Province,[4] so that the Friendship of Mr. Townshend[5] can be of little service to me on this Occasion, as I know he will not take

[1] The recipient of this letter must have been Elizabeth Gunning, the Duchess of Hamilton, and of Argyll. She married in 1752 the Sixth Duke of Hamilton, who died in 1758. In 1759 she married the fifth Duke of Argyll. For more data concerning her, see *The Complete Peerage*, London, vol. vi (1926), 270–1. See also Horace Bleackley's *The Story of a Beautiful Duchess*, London, 1908, which contains four of her portraits. It seems that she passed on this letter from Smollett to the Earl of Shelburne, who sent her a reply (Anderson, 189).

[2] What is conveyed or expressed.

[3] This nephew of Smollett was Major Alexander Telfer. (Knapp, 268, 294.)

[4] William Petty, Earl of Shelburne, and first Marquis of Lansdowne. For Smollett's applications for consulships, and for the Earl of Shelburne's opposition, see Knapp, 271–2. See also Letter 89.

[5] Charles Townshend (1725–67) Chancellor of the Exchequer in William Pitt's administration. See Sir Lewis Namier's *Charles Townshend His Character and Career*, The Leslie Stephen Lecture, 1959 (Cambridge, 1959). Smollett referred to Townshend in *Humphry Clinker* (Letter of J. Melford, London, 5 June).

any step that looks like interfering in the Department of another Minister. I would much rather owe my success to the Interest and good offices of Your Grace, which, if I am so happy as to attain, I shall ever exert my best Endeavours to approve myself not unworthy of your Protection, and eagerly seize every opportunity of showing with what Zeal and Attachment I have the Honour to be,

Madam,
Your Grace's most obedient and
most humble servant
T⁵ Smollett

Bath, Jany 17, 1767

Address: not available. *Source:* MS. in NLS. *First Printing:* in this edition.

Letter 100

To John Moore

Bath, Feby. 8, 1767

Dear John Moore,

I have been for some weeks resolved to write you an account of my Health, about which I know your friendly sollicitude, but what hastens the Execution of my Purpose is a Letter I recieved last Post from Commissary Smollett,[1] desiring me to recommend a poor Cousin of ours to your Countenance and Protection. Her name is Mrs. Macarthur, sister to the Laird of Craignish, who is my first Cousin.[2] This unfortunate Gentlewoman married one Macarthur who had a small estate in the Highlands,[3] which having squandered away, he made his Retreat to Jamaica, leaving his wife destitute with a Child upon her Hands. In this Emergency she had virtue enough to study Midwifery under Dr. Young at Ed⁵[4] who, I am told, has given ample Testimonials of her capacity; and she is represented to me as a Person of unblemished Character. She has, it

[1] Smollett's cousin James.

[2] Smollett's aunt Eleanor married Dugald Campbell of Craignish in 1718. (See Irving, 1760, p. 342.) Smollett's first cousin must have been Dugald Campbell, Jr., presumably M.P. for Argylshire in 1754. See *Universal Magazine,* xiv, (1754), 253. For Craignish, see Chambers, 157–8, footnote.

[3] This Macarthur remains unidentified.

[4] Probably Thomas Young, M.D. See Dr. John Glaister's *Dr. William Smellie and his Contemporaries* (Glasgow, 1894), 282.

(129)

seems, resolved to settle at Glasgow and there exercise her Profession. I need say no more, knowing as I do, that you will have a proper Regard to the Interest I take in her Concerns; and that if you find her properly qualified, he will encourage her as much as your own Views and Connexions may permit. So much for Mrs. Macarthur, and now for Dr. Smollett. You must remember the miserable way in which I was at parting from you in August last. At my return to Bath, I caught Cold, in consequence of which my Rheumatic Pains retired, and the Disorder in my Breast recurred, namely an Orthopnoea,[1] with an ugly Cough and spitting, exclusive of a slow fever from which I had never been free. But these Symptoms gave me little Disturbance in comparison with the ulcer on my fore arm, which continued to spread untill it occupied the whole space from about three inches above the wrist to the Ball of the Thumb so that I was intirely deprived of the use of my right hand, and the Inflammation and Pain daily increased. In the Beginning of November, it was supposed to be cancerous. At that period I could not sleep without an opiate; my Fever became continual; my appetite failed; and the Rheumatism again invaded me from the neck to the Heel. In a word, I despaired of ever seeing the End of Winter, and every night when I went to bed, fervently wished that I might be dead before morning. In this comfortable situation, I consulted with Messrs. Middleton[2] and Sharp,[3] the two most eminent Surgeons in England, who were then and are still at Bath. I had my Hand dressed before them and proposed a course for the cure, which they approved. I forthwith began to dress the sore with double mecurial ointment made without Turpentine. I took a dose of Van Sweeten's[4] solution of corrosive sublimate every morning, and drank a Quart of strong Decoct. Sarsae[5] every day. On the second day of this Regimen the matter was much mended, and the Pain considerable abated. In one week I was quite free of

[1] A form of asthma in which breathing is possible only in an upright position (*OED*).

[2] David Middleton, one of the King's surgeons. In 1763, John Wilkes, having refused the services of Caesar Hawkins, Sergeant-Surgeon to George III, and Dr. William Heberdeen, summoned William Duncan and David Middleton, also Sergeant Surgeon to George III, both Scotsmen. See Horace Bleackley's *Life of John Wilkes* (1917), 142; and *Gentleman's Magazine*, xxxiii (1763), 616–17.

[3] Samuel Sharp (1700–78), a prominent London surgeon, and friend of David Garrick. He was the author of several medical books, and *Letters from Italy* (1766), which led Sterne to call him 'Mundungus', and which infuriated Giuseppe Baretti, author of *An Account of Manners and Customs of Italy* (1767). For an extract from a review of Sharp's book in the *Critical Review* (Oct. 1766), see Noyes, 219.

[4] Baron Van Swieten.   [5] Decoction of sarsaparilla (Letter 101).

the Fever and Rheumatism, and my appetite returned in full
perfection. In ten days I left off taking the sublimate, for, by this
time the ulcer was almost closed, and in another week skinned over.
It continues still hard and scaly; but the Cicatrix[1] seems quite
firm; and I can now use my Hand almost as well as ever. I still
drink the Decoction and never stirred out of my House 'till
yesterday, when I ventured out in a Chair and got a cursed Cold
                                      this
which I find will produce an ugly fit of the asthma; ~~which~~ [*sic*], however, I will bear without repining. In a word, my cure is looked
upon as something supernatural; and I must own that I now find
myself better in Health and spirits than I have been at any time
these seven years. Had I been as well in Summer, I should have
exquisitely enjoyed my Expedition to Scotland which was productive of nothing to me but Misery and Disgust.[2] Between Friends, I
am now convinced that my Brain was in some measure affected;
for I had a kind of *Coma vigil* upon me from April to November
without Intermission. In consideration of these Circumstances, I
know you will forgive all my Peevishness and Discontent; and tell
Mrs. Moore, to whom I present my most cordial Respects, that
with regard to me she has as yet seen nothing but the wrong side of
the Tapestry.[3] Pray remember me kindly to your Brother in law
Mr. Simpson,[4] to Drs. Stevenson[5] and Douglas,[6] to honest Robin
Urie,[7] and all my Glasgow friends. Write to me with your first

[1] Scar or seam of a healed sore.

[2] Dr. John Moore in his 'Life of Dr. Smollett', *The Works of Tobias Smollett,
M.D.*, 8 vols. (London, 1797), i, p. clxxiv, commented on his physical ailments
while in Glasgow in 1766 as follows: 'These disorders confined him much to his
chamber, but did not prevent his conversation being highly entertaining when
he joined society.'

[3] For the early Spanish uses of this tapestry metaphor (or simile), see Samuel
Putnam's translation of Cervantes' *Don Quixote* (The Viking Press, New York,
1949), 1028, n. 29. In Smollett's translation of *Don Quixote* 2 vols. (London,
1755), ii, 403, is the following: 'a translation from one languge [*sic*] to
another, excepting always those sovereign tongues the Greek and Latin, is, in
my opinion, like the wrong side of Flemish tapestry.' See also a critical comment
which appeared in a review, almost certainly by Smollett, of *The Peregrinations
of Jeremiah Grant, Esq; the West-Indian* in the *Critical Review*, xv (1763), 18.

[4] James Simson (1729–77), brother of Jean Simson, Dr. Moore's wife, and son
of Robert Simson, professor first of theology, and later of mathematics. James
Simson was the partner of John Baird in a small banking firm, which experienced a failure in 1772. He was also, along with Dr. Moore, a member of the
Hodge-Podge Club.

[5] Dr. Alexander Stevenson of Dolgain, Professor of Medicine at the University of Glasgow, 1766–89. See Alexander Duncan, *Memorials of the Faculty of
Physicians and Surgeons of Glasgow 1599–1850* (Glasgow, 1896), 258.

[6] Dr. Colin Douglas (Alexander Duncan, *op. cit.*, 122, 259).

[7] See Letter 20, n. 4, p. 32.

convenience, directing to Dr. Smollett in Gay-street, Bath,[1] and believe me to be with the warmest affection and Esteem,

Dear John Moore,
Your much obliged humble Servt.,
T: Smollett

Address: To Mr. John Moore Surgeon in Glasgow, North Britain. *Source:* MS. of PTS. *First Printing:* Partly in Moore, I, clxxv. Completely in Noyes, 98–101.

Letter 101

To Dr. [William] Hunter

Bath, Feby. 24, 1767

Dear Sir,

I would rather be found guilty of Intrusion than be suspected of Ingratitude, and therefore I trouble you with this Intimation as in Duty bound that you may know I am still crawling on the face of the Earth, and that I am even in a Condition to crawl on all four as dressing it with the use of my right hand is in some measure restored by the use of [*sic*] mercurial ointment,[2] and by Dint of Drinking the Decoction of Sarsaparilla.[3] About three months ago, I was verily persuaded that the cursed ulcer on my Forearm was become cancerous, and that the sore was a Judgement of God upon me for the ridiculous use I had made of that wretched member in writing such a Heap of absurdities in the Course of my Authorial Probation.[4] At present the Part is skinned over but looks very shabby and leprous, and the Lord knows how soon it may break out again. Meanwhile, I can sit without agony and sleep without an opiate, and I am very ready to compound with[5] Providence for the Priviledge of these happy

[1] Gay Street, near the centre of Bath, runs from Queen Square to The Circus.
[2] In Letter 100, Smollett referred to using this ointment.
[3] In Letter 100, Smollett referred to using this decoction.
[4] Period of publication prior to an author's successful status. In his *Dictionary*, under *probation*, Johnson cited the following: 'I suffer many things as an author militant, whereof, in your days of *probation* you have been a sharer. Pope to Swift.' See *The Correspondence of Alexander Pope*, ed. George Sherburn, 5 vols. (Oxford Clarendon Press, 1956), i, 342. It is possible that among the 'absurdities' to which Smollett alluded there were imprints of conundrums, published anonymously before *Roderick Random*. He was, according to Dr. James Grainger in his satirical *Letter to Tobias Smollett, M.D.* (London, 1759), 6, 'endowed with . . . Conundrum Genius'.
[5] To compromise with, or to settle with.

Exemptions. After all, it is a long time since I had any other than negative Enjoyments, and indeed I have almost forgot what positive Pleasure is. I am almost stupefied with ill Health, Loss of memory, Confinement and Solitude, and I believe in my Conscience the Circulation would have stopped of itself if it was not every now and then stimulated by the Stings of my Grub street Friends, who attack me in the public Papers.[1] Sometimes I am baited as a Dunce, then a ministerial Hireling, then a Jacobite, then a rancorous Knave, then a Liar, Quack and assassin. A Dunce I partly believe myself to be, but as to the other Epithets I humbly concieve they are missapplied, for even Mr. Secretary Conway[2] himself will never be able to persuade me either that I am a Jacobite, or that I ever exhibited the outward Signs and Symptoms of that Infection. Long Life to those great Men! And I pray God they may become Saints in Heaven. For my Part, even after their Canonization, I shall rather than trouble them on their Thrones of Beatification, address my Prayers to the spirit of honest George Macaulay, who I know will do me all the service in his power, notwithstanding the Discrepancy betwixt my notions of Government and those of his learned spouse,[3] who, I am told, is now all masculine above low water mark. Pray excuse this Nonsense as a Thing of course from,

Dear Doctor,

Your much obliged humble Servt.,

T.⁵ Smollett

Address: To Doctor Hunter at his House in Jermyn Street[4] London. *Source:* MS. in RCS. *First Printing:* Probably Noyes, 101–3.

[1] All of these attacks have not yet been identified. For several of them, printed in 1766 in the *London Chronicle*, see Noyes, 221.

[2] Henry Seymour Conway (1721–95), Secretary of State under Rockingham in 1765. His brother, the Marquis of Hertford, helped Smollett regain his books held for a time by the French government (Letter 94).

[3] Catharine Macaulay (1733–91), also known as Catharine Macaulay Graham after her second marriage. She was a radical English historian and an extraordinary person, widely publicized. For an excellent account (illustrated) of her life and career, see Lucy Martin Donnelly's 'The Celebrated Mrs. Macaulay', in *The William and Mary Quarterly*, 3rd Ser., vol. vi, No. 2 (Apr. 1949), [173]–207.

[4] Jermyn Street is located on the east side of St. James's Street, parallel with Piccadilly. Here Dr. William Hunter resided until 1770.

Letter 102

To Robert Cotton[1]

Bath, May 18, 1768

Dear Sir,

I have a very gratefull sense of your Kindness to Miss Curry[2] when she was lately in London, and think myself much obliged to you and good Mrs. Cotton for all your Expressions of Friendship and Regard. I shall never forget the chearfull Hours I have passed in your Company; and I regret very much my being at such a Distance as not only interrupts our Society but prevents me from offering my advice, such as it is, to Mrs. Cotton, in the state of whose Health I take a Sincere Concern.

You desire to know the method of converting the white of an Egg into a substance resembling Amber. You have nothing to do but to peel off the white of a hard boiled Egg and let it lie upon some shelf for four or five months, when by the Influence of the air it becomes of the Colour and Consistence of Amber, and may (like it) be chipped and used in fineering.[3] I have often thought that by incorporating a number of whites together, and dropping into them a Drop or two of the oil of amber one might procure a large Mass and model it into different shapes for Snuff boxes, Cane Heads etc; and this being properly consolidated by boiling and afterwards left to dry, would have not only the appearance and Consistence, but even the Smell of genuine Amber. Perhaps this Process may require many repeated Experiments before it is brought to Perfection, but as you have a Turn for natural curiosities, I know you will not begrudge your Labour, especially as it is attended with very little Expense, and will not take up much of your Time. I hear Mrs. Cotton[4] intends to try the Effect of a Sea Voyage to Newcastle, and I very much approve of her Intention, for I know nothing more likely to set her up.

Pray, remember me to our friend Halford,[5] who I hear is still in

---

[1] Robert Salusbury Cotton (?–1790), F.R.S., a London apothecary. See Reginald Blunt, *Memoirs of Gerald Blunt of Chelsea, His Family and Forebears . . . including . . . Forssteen and Cotton Memorials by Jane Mary Craig* (London, 1911), *passim*.

[2] Anne Curry, who married George W. Renner in Florence in 1769. Smollett and his wife were witnesses at this wedding (Knapp, 283–4).

[3] Veneering.

[4] *Née* Alison Robertson, daughter of James Robertson of Glasgow (Reginald Blunt, *op. cit.*).

[5] Probably Oakley Halford, who lived at No. 3 Cheyne Walk, Chelsea, 1748–81 (Walter H. Godfrey, *The Parish of Chelsea Part I . . . Being the Second Volume of the Survey of London . . . (c.* 1909), 36).

To David Hume, 31 August 1768

a single state. If I had a little Health and spirits I would write a Ballad upon him entituled *the old Batchelor's Ditty*. If he will clap on a Bag wig and bit of Lace and come down to Bath, it shall go hard but I will buckle him for Life. Here is his neighbour Major Macdonald,[1] but he does not seem to profit much by the waters. Yet he is fat and fair, and his Tongue goes as fast as ever. I shall be very happy to hear from you when you are at Leisure. My wife and Miss Curry and Fanny[2] join me in our best wishes for you and Mrs. Cotton and Family. I desire you will keep out of these cursed Riots,[3] and believe that I am with very great Esteem and affection,

My dear Sir,

Your very humble Servt.,

T: Smollett

Address: To Robt Cotton Esqr at his House in Crown Court Westminster London. *Source:* MS. in CPL. *First Printing:* By Knapp, 'More Smollett Letters', *MLN*, xlviii (1933), 247–9.

Letter 103
[To David Hume][4]

London, Augt. 31, 1768

Dear Sir,

Perhaps I overrate my own Consequence when I presume to recommend to your acquaintance and good offices the Bearer, Capt. Robt. Stobo,[5] a man, whose very extraordinary Services and Sufferings in America have merited and obtained the most ample and honourable Testimonials which he will gladly submit to your Perusal. I can safely say from my own Knowledge that he is not less modest and sensible in the conversation and occurrencies of

[1] One Major M'Donald is on a list of those who, like Smollett, donated oddities to Don Saltero's Coffee House in Chelsea (Walter H. Godfrey, *op. cit.*, 63).

[2] Frances Lascelles, granddaughter of Mrs. Elizabeth Leaver, Smollett's mother-in-law (Letter 13, n. 2, p. 20).

[3] In the newspapers of May 1768, are accounts of the attempts of rioters to free John Wilkes from the King's Bench Prison.

[4] David Hume (1711–1776), the distinguished Scottish philosopher and historian.

[5] Robert Stobo (1727–*c*.1772). For data concerning Stobo, see Kahrl, *passim*; and Kahrl, 'Captain Robert Stobo', *The Virginia Magazine of History and Biography*, xlix (1941), 141–51 and 254–68. See also Martz, *passim*, and Robert C. Alberts, *The Most Extraordinary Adventures of Major Robert Stobo* (Boston, 1965). Stobo was a source of some of the characteristics of Smollett's Lismahago in *Humphry Clinker*.

civil Life than enterprizing and indefatigable in his military Capacity. All these good qualities united to an extensive Knowledge of our american Concerns cannot fail to engage the Friendship and Regard of Mr. David Hume, from what quarter soever they may come recommended.

With respect to myself, I am sorry I cannot have the Pleasure of taking Leave of you in person before I go into perpetual Exile. I sincerely wish you all Health and Happiness. In whatever part of the Earth it may be my Fate to reside, I shall always remember with Pleasure, and recapitulate with Pride, the friendly Intercourse[1] I have maintained with one of the best men, and, undoubtedly, the best writer of the age if any Judgement in distinguishing either Character or Capacity may be allowed to,

Dear Sir,

Your very humble Servt.,

T$_S$ Smollett

Nos Patrium fugimus—tu Tityre, lentus sub umbrâ formosam resonare doces Amaryllida silvas.[2]

Address: Not available. *Source:* MS. in RSE. *First Printing:* In John Hill Burton's *Life and Correspondence of David Hume* (Edinburgh, 1846), ii, 418.

Letter 104
To Caleb Whitefoord[3]

Monte-Nero, May 18, 1770

My dear Sir,

You could not have made me a more agreable Present than the Papers I received by the hands of our good friend, Dr. Armstrong.[4]

---

[1] By the term, 'friendly intercourse', Smollett implies that he and Hume had written to each other, at least more than once. However, this letter and Hume's reply are the only ones that are located.

[2] See Virgil's *Eclogue*, I, 4–5. Smollett apparently quoted these lines from memory, as Virgil wrote, at the end of line 4, *in umbra* instead of *sub umbrâ*. Translation: We hasten away from our country. You, Tityrus, at ease in the shade, teach the woods to resound with the name of Amaryllis.

[3] Caleb Whitefoord (1734–1810) F.R.S. and S.A., wine merchant and littérateur. He was a friend of Goldsmith and Benjamin Franklin. For his literary interests and his improvement of cross-readings, see *The Whitefoord Papers*, ed. W. A. S. Hewins (Oxford, Clarendon Press, 1898), XXI–XXIX. For a sample of his cross-readings, see Noyes, 225, and George Irwin, 'Whitefoord is our Leader', *TLS* (28 Jan. 1965), 72.

[4] See Letter 7, n. 3, p. 11.

TOBIAS SMOLLETT, *c.* 1770
By an unknown Italian artist

To Caleb Whitefoord, 18 May 1770

Some of the Pieces I had read with great Pleasure in one of your
evening papers; but my Satisfaction is much increased by knowing
you are the Author, for, without Flattery, I really think these
Fourteen Letters[1] contain more sense, spirit, Wit and Humour than
all I have as yet seen written on the other side of the question; and
I am fully persuaded that if you had two or three Coadjutors of
equal Talents to play to one another's hands, and keep up the Ball
of Argument and Ridicule, you would actually at the long run,
either shame or laugh the people out of their absurd Infatuation.
Your Ideas of Characters and things so exactly tally with mine that
I cannot help flattering myself so far as to imagine I should have
expressed my Sentiments in the same manner on the same Subjects,
had I been disposed to make them public, supposing still that my
ability corresponded with my ambition. I hope you will not dis-
continue your Endeavours to represent Faction and False patriot-
ism[2] in their true Colours, tho' I believe the Ministry[3] little deserves
that any *man of Genius* should draw his pen in their Defence. They
seem to inherit the absurd Stoicism of Lord Bute,[4] who set himself
up as a Pillory to be pelted by all the Blackguards of England, upon
the Supposition that they would grow tired and leave off. I don't
find that your Ministers take any pains even to vindicate their
moral Characters from the foulest Imputation; and I would never
desire a stronger proof of a bad Heart than a total Disregard of
Reputation.[5] A late nobleman who had been a member of several
administrations owned to me that one good Writer was of more
Importance to the Government than twenty placemen[6] in the
House of Commons.

I don't know when I shall have an opportunity of transmitting

[1] These letters remain unidentified. They probably appeared in the *Public
Advertiser* (*c.* 1769–70).

[2] The political policies of John Wilkes and his supporters.

[3] It is uncertain whether Smollett referred to the ministry of the Duke of
Grafton, or of his successor, Lord North.

[4] John Stuart, third Earl of Bute (1713–92), Prime Minister, 1762–3. His
personal relations with Smollett remain obscure, as no correspondence between
them has been discovered. Bute was the son-in-law of Lady Mary Wortley
Montagu. See *The Complete Letters of Lady Mary Wortley Montagu*, ed. Robert
Halsband 3 vols., (Oxford, Clarendon Press, 1965–7), *passim*.

[5] In a copy of Robert Anderson's *Life of Tobias Smollett*, 4th ed. (1803),
presented by Anderson to John Ramsay, there is a manuscript note (p. 132),
perhaps by Ramsay, stating that this sentence is 'The old remark of Tacitus',
and referring to a line from this Roman poet (*Annales*, IV, 38): *nam contemptu
famae contemni virtutes*, which translated means 'To despise fame is to despise
merit'.

[6] Those who hold an appointment in the service of the Sovereign or State,
usually in a hostile sense (*OED*).

the papers to Mr. Udny ;[1] neither do I know in what part of Italy he resides. I should have sent them by Dr. Armstrong to Rome, had I read your Letter before he set out, but as he stayed at Leghorne only to dine with me, I did not open your Pacquet 'till he was gone. However, I shall not fail to comply with your Directions as soon as possible. I am at present rusticated on the side of a mountain/that overlooks the sea[2] in the neighbourhood of Leghorne, a most romantic and salutary Situation, where I should be happy in receiving another such mark of your charity, and good will; and if there is any thing in Tuscany that you desire, I beg you will without Ceremony put it in my power to oblige you. Pray, who is *old Slyboots*?[3] Is not *Junius* supposed to be *Burke*?[4] What is become of *Mrs. Macaulay*?[5] They say she has been obliged to retire, for what reason I know not. Do pray throw away half an hour in giving me the political Anecdotes of the Times, and direct a Monsr. Monsr. Smollett chez Monsr. Renner, Négotiant a Livourne.[6] In the meantime wishing you Every Comfort and Consolation that this rascally Age affords, I am with great affection and Esteem,

Dear Sir,

Your very humble Servt.,

T: Smollett

Address: To Caleb Whitefoord, Esq. at his House in Craven Street, Strand, London, Inghilterra. *Source:* MS. of PTS. *First Printing:* Moore, I, clxxxv–clxxxvii.

[1] The British consul, John Udney. In *The St. James's Chronicle* (9–11 Nov. 1769) is the following statement : 'A letter from Leghorn, dated October 20 says "Mr. Dick and Mr. Udney, English consuls, the one in this city, and the other at Venice, have received orders from their Court . . . to observe a perfect neutrality in the war between Russia and the Ottoman Porte."' John Udney was a friend of Horace Walpole.

[2] Monte Nero, a few miles from Livorno, on the south side of which Smollett lived.

[3] Old Slyboots was a *nom de plume* of James Scott, D.D. (*DNB*). Some articles signed Old Slyboots which had appeared in the *London Chronicle* during Mar., Apr., and May 1770 were printed in *Fugitive Political Essays* (London, 1770).

[4] In 1770, many thought that 'Junius' might have been Edmund Burke. Possibly Whitefoord could have identified 'Junius' (Noyes, 227).

[5] See Letter 101, n. 3, p. 133.

[6] George William Renner, probably born at Bremen, Germany (Knapp, *passim*). Among the papers in Smollett's trunk sent after his death to Philadelphia was a document signed in 1745 by Theodoro Primo, then King of Corsica, appointing Renner as consul of Livorno. This document is in the Historical Society of Pennsylvania (Du Simitière Papers, 967, F). For Theodor B. von Neuhof, King of Corsica, see Frederick A. Pottle, *James Boswell The Earlier Years 1740–1769*, (New York, 1966), *passim*.

Letter 105
To Alexander Telfer of Symington[1]

Leghorne, Jany 9, 1771

Dear Squire,

I wrote last week by the Post, in answer to yours that transmitted the Commissary's[2] Intimation concerning his propos'd improvements; and I give you this additional trouble to introduce the Bearer, Mr. Cochrane,[3] to your Acquaintance.

He is a very worthy and accomplished young Surgeon who purposes (I think) to settle in your Neighbourhood, and I can very safely recommend him to your good offices and Friendship. He came to this Country with Sir David Murray[4] last summer, who died of a Consumption a few days after his arrival so that I have had sufficient time to be acquainted with Mr. Cochrane's Character, which is really respectable. On Tuesday we were alarmed by an Earthquake[5] which visited us in repeated shocks, some of which were violent and terrible. Mr. Cochrane can inform you of the particulars, as they don't seem to have greatly disturbed his Intellects, whatever effects they may have produced on the People of Leghorne, great part of whom fled from the City, some on Board the Ships and Vessels in the harbour and Canals, and some to the Country.

I could hardly keep my own Family within Doors, but for my own part I thought it was better to run some small risque of being smother'd quietly in my own warm bed than expose myself to certain Death from the Damps of a dark Winter night, while the cold was excessive. The bearer can also inform you of the circumstances of my health and manner of living (if you desire to know them), and being a *Dilletante* in Musick, will communicate his Ideas on that subject to you and George Cowper.[6]

I repeat my Complts. to Mrs. Telfer, to your Mother,[7] to

---

[1] Smollett's nephew, and partly the original of Smollett's Jery Melford in *Humphry Clinker*. Alexander Telfer was the ancestor of the present Telfer Smolletts of Cameron House on Loch Lomond.

[2] Smollett's cousin, Commissary James Smollett. See Letter 27.

[3] Unidentified.

[4] Only partially identified. See Noyes, 228–9.

[5] For an account of the earthquakes at Leghorn given by the Consul, Sir John Dick, see *Curiosities of a Scots Charta Chest 1600–1800*, ed. The Hon[ble] Mrs. Atholl Forbes (Edinburgh, 1897), 240.

[6] Unidentified.

[7] Smollett's sister, Jane.

Extract from a letter to John Hunter, 9 January 1771

Capt. James,[1] to Jeanny[2] and all friends, and am without flummery,[3]

Dear Laird,
Yours always,
T.ˢ Smollett

My address is Monsr. Monsr. Smollett chez Monsr. Renner,[4] Négotiant a Livorne en Toscane.

Address: On the manuscript copy of this letter is the following: 'Dr. Smollet to Alexr. Telfer of Symington Esqr. brought by Mr. Cochrane'. *Source:* Manuscript 'Coppy' of PTS, not in Smollett's handwriting. *First Printing:* Partially in *Scots Magazine*, lxvii (1805), 331–2, and completely, except Smollett's address, in Noyes, 107–8.

Letter 106

Extract from a letter to John Hunter[5]

Leghorn, January 9, 1771

With respect to myself, I have nothing to say but that if I can prevail upon my wife to execute my last will, you shall receive my poor carcase in a box, after I am dead, to be placed among your rarities. I am already so dry and emaciated that I may pass for an Egyptian mummy without any other preparation than some pitch and painted linen, unless you think I may deserve the denomination of a curiosity in my own character, I mean that of

Your old friend,
and affectionate humble servant,
T.ˢ Smollett

Address: Not available. *Source:* MS. not located. *First Printing: Scots Magazine*, lxvii (1805), 331–2.

[1] A younger brother of Alexander Telfer of Symington.
[2] Possibly a niece of Smollett.
[3] A trifling compliment.
[4] For Renner, see Letter 104, n. 6, p. 138.
[5] For John Hunter, see Letter 95, n. 2, p. 123. The complete letter, of which this is a fragment, has not been found. No other letters from Smollett to John Hunter are available.

Letter 107
To George William Renner[1]

Lucca Baths,[2] Wednesday, Augt. 21 [1771]

Dear Sir,

I was favoured with yours last night, and take this opportunity of answering it, as I am determined to be with you as soon as possible. We shall Set out from hence on Monday morning and lie at Pisa, and on Tuesday we propose to take pot Luck with you at Leghorne so that we may proceed to the Giardino[3] in the Evening. Meanwhile I must beg the favour of you to write Mr. Favilla[4] that I shall be at Lucca next Monday, and that I shall have occasion for Twenty Zecchines,[5] as I should not care to be run to the last Paul.[6] He may then take my order upon you for the money, and I will pay him the amount of what he has laid out in our behalf since we left Leghorn. You will therefore desire him to have the acct. ready to Settle.

The Baggage we shall Send to Leghorne by the Canal; and when we arrive we shall be able to judge what must be forwarded to the Giardino, where I hope you will remember to make Some Provision of wine. We shall have the best part of a Barrel to our friend Domenicho,[7] who has not yet received the printed Cotton, but I suppose it will come to hand this day or to-morrow.

Pray, remember us to Nanny and Kitty,[8] Capt. St. Barbe[9] and all friends, and excuse this fresh Trouble from,

Dear Sir,
yours always,
T: Smollett

Address: A Monsieur Monsr. Renner, Négotiant, à Livourne. See *Port Folio* Philadelphia, I (1806), 199. *Source:* MS. not located. *First Printing: Port Folio* i, (1806), 199.

[1] For George William Renner, see Letter 104, n. 6, p. 138.
[2] Lucca Baths is about fifteen miles north-west of Lucca. For a detailed map revealing the eighteenth-century routes from Lucca to Livorno, see Antonio Cocchi, *Dei Bogni di Pisa* (Firenzi, 1750), (A copy in Harvard University Library). See also Noyes, 231–2.
[3] The name of the villa where Smollett lived on the side of Monte Nero.
[4] Unidentified.
[5] A sequin was an Italian gold coin worth about nine shillings (*OED*).
[6] An obsolete Italian silver coin worth about fivepence sterling. See Noyes, 231.
[7] Unidentified.
[8] Perhaps George Renner's daughters.
[9] Unidentified.

ADDENDUM

To Provost Macaulay, 14 October 1753

Letter 108[1]

To Provost Macaulay

Chelsea, Oct. 14 1753

Dear Sir,

When I reflect upon the generous Hospitality and warmth of Friendship with which I have been treated by my worthy friend Provost Macaulay,[2] I consider every moment that I delay to express my acknowledgement, as a fresh Breach of Gratitude and Duty. Indeed, Sir, you may believe me when I assure you that no Length of Time, no vicissitude of Life, no interruption of Correspondence shall ever be able to eraze or even to impair the Impressions which your Kindness hath left upon my Heart, or diminish that perfect Esteem and Regard which I in common with all Mankind, have for your Character and Benevolence. But enough of this Profession[3] which tho' the genuine overflowings of an Heart that disdains to dissemble, is at best but an Expedient[4] which the worst of men can use for the worst of purposes.

I arrived in perfect Health at Chelsea, after a Journey of Twelve days [Ms. torn, possibly two words missing] I was extremely happy in the Company of my fellow Travellers; for, you must know it was Good Fortune to fall in with Mr. Ronald Crawford[5] with his wife and her sister Miss Forbes, and Mr. Brown of Blackford[6]; and we were afterwards overtaken by Mr. James Vietch [?Veitch][7] and his Sister, so that we clubbed our Proportions[8] for a joint Stock[9] and lived together with great Elegance and Harmony. The Ladies

---

[1] The date of this letter is that of Smollett's return to Chelsea after his first trip back to Scotland. I have not seen the manuscript. It was read by Claire Lamont of Somerville College, Oxford, who sent me two xeroxes, on both of which some words are not visible. However, having read Claire Lamont's recent article, 'William Collins's "Ode On The Popular Superstitions of the Highlands of Scotland"—a newly recovered Manuscript' in *The Review Of English Studies*, xix, [135]–147, I am convinced that she is a reliable scholar, and I am glad to accept as accurate her typed copy of the manuscript for which I am very grateful.

[2] Archibald Macaulay, Lord Provost of Edinburgh. I have not discovered his possible relationship to Dr. George Macaulay.

[3] Declaration of an opinion.

[4] Means to an end.

[5] Unidentified.

[6] Unidentified.

[7] Unidentified.

[8] United our monetary shares.   [9] Combined fund.

(142)

were as agreable Creatures as ever I knew, and the Gentlemen good Companions who loved their Bottle which I assure you, was not spared upon the Road. I found your Son and Daughter well and happy and to Mrs. Gregory[1] did I deliver the Book which was intrusted to my Care by Mrs. Macaulay[2] to whom I beg leave to offer my Sincere Thanks for all her Favours, and in particular for her last Present which I shall carefully peruse and preserve with the utmost Veneration, as a friendly Token of her humane Concern for the wellfare of my eternal Soul which is undoubtedly of infinitely more importance than all other Considerations.

I must employ you to present my best Respects to Mr. and Mrs. Frazer[3], to Provost Drummond,[4] the Commissary and Mrs. Smollett,[5] and to Mr. Macmillan[6] whom I hope [you will be so good as to remind of poor Willy Campbell's[7] Case which is truly deplorable. You have been engaged in many offices of Humanity, and I believe few objects ever deserved your attention more than that wretched Man who is really in Extremity, both with regard to health and Circumstances.

That you may long continue to exert that Beneficence which I know is your Delight and be a Blessing to the society among which you live, I sincerely and earnestly wish, and intreat of Heaven, while I subscribe myself with inviolable Truth and affection

> Dear Sir,
> Your most obd.[t] and much obliged humble Servt.,
> T.[s] Smollett

[2–3 words torn away] who are well offer their kind Compliments to you and good Mrs. Macaulay to whom I hope you will also make [2–3 words missing] as to my favourite Miss Moody[8] for whom I hope all Happiness is in Store.

Address: Not available. *Source:* MS. belonging to Colonel A. E. Cameron, Aldourie Castle, Inverness, Scotland. I am grateful to him for allowing it to be published. *First Printing:* in this edition.

[1] Unidentified.
[2] Undoubtedly the provost's wife.
[3] Provost Macaulay's daughter and son-in-law according to Claire Lamont.
[4] George Drummond, Lord Provost of Edinburgh. See *DNB*, and Robert Chambers' *A Biographical Dictionary of Eminent Scotsmen* (4 vols., Glasgow, 1835), II, 133–36. For George Drummond's brother, Alexander Drummond, consul at Aleppo, Smollett prepared for the press an interesting book of travels. See Knapp, 160, 163, 250, n.
[5] Commissary Smollett was the cousin of Tobias Smollett.
[6] Unidentified.
[7] Unidentified.
[8] Unidentified.

INDEX

S is an abbreviation for Tobias Smollett

Index

Index

Simile, 'like an owl in an Ivy Bush', 106 and n. 7

Simpson [Simson] James, 131, n. 4

Simson, Miss Jean, 57, n. 1

Simson, John, Professor of Divinity, 57, n. 1

Simson, Robert, father of James Simson, 131, n. 4

Sinclair, Capt. David, 69

Smalet, 43

Smeaton, Oliphant, *Tobias Smollett*, xvi

Smellie, Dr. William, xvi, 15 and n. 3, 17 and n. 1, 27, n. 1, 32 and n. 6, 62, n. 4

Smith, Richard of Burlington, New Jersey, North America, 112 and n. 1, and n. 2

Smith, Robert [Bob], xvii, 5 and n. 3, 10 and n. 3, 35 and n. 10, 38 and n. 4, 39 and n. 1

Smollett, Commissary, and Mrs., 143 and n. 5

Smollett, Elizabeth, S's daughter, 36, n. 5, 84 and n. 11, 113 and n. 6, 117 and n. 2

Smollett, James, 1, 38, n. 3

Smollett, Sir James, 116, n. 1

Smollett, Jane, 139, n. 7

Smollett, Tobias—

His major literary and social activities, his opinions and problems

Academy of Belles Lettres, attempt to establish it, 46

Amanuensis, his, 57

Army in Portugal, attempt to be its physician, 108

Attacks in print on Alexander H. Campbell, 21–6; on Admiral Charles Knowles, *see* Knowles

Attacks on S, verbal, 95, n. 3, 133 and n. 1

Assistance, financial, for Mr. Hamilton, 51

Assistance, literary, for William Huggins, 54

Character, his own in 1762, a remarkable confession of, 107

Chelsea, approval of persons there, 42; criticism of persons there, 33; his friends and neighbours there, *see* John Lewis, Capt. Robert Mann, and Dr. Alexander Reid; tributes received there, 97 and n. 2

Church of England, his consideration of it, 73 and n. 2

Consulships offered and sought for, at Leghorn, 111, n. 3; at Madrid, 83, n. 4, 111; at Marseilles, 111; at Nice, 111 and n. 3, 128

Descriptions, literary, of Cemeleon, Italy, 123–4; of Nice, 121–2

Desire to stop writing, 73

Doctor of Medicine, degree received in 1749, 112 and n. 6

Financial income from East Indies, West Indies and Scotland, and financial problems, 28, 40 and n. 2, 41 and n. 1, 45, 49, 62–3, 68 and n. 4

Friends, *see* Dr. John Armstrong, Charles Bell, Robert Cotton, Dr. Robert Dick, John Home [Hume], David Hume, Dr. William Hunter, Dr. George Macaulay, Daniel MacKercher, Dr. John Moore, John Ritchie, and Robert Smith

Gift of venison received, 71 and n. 5

Glasgow, prigs of, 39 and n. 5

Health, many details concerning his complicated illness and his efforts to avoid or control it, 82 and n. 1, 83, 101, 106 and n. 4, 107, 108, 109, 120–1, 124, 126 and n. 3, 128, 130–1, 131, n. 2, 132–3; his *Coma vigil*, 131. His plans for bathing in the sea, 107 and 119, and horseback-riding, 107

Index

Index